Youth Participatory Arts, Learning and Social Transformation

Youth Participatory Arts, Learning and Social Transformation

Engaging People, Place and Context with Big hART

By

Peter Wright and Barry Down

with Scott Rankin

Foreword by François Matarasso

BRILL

SENSE

LEIDEN | BOSTON

Cover illustration: Photograph by Christopher Saunders

All chapters in this book have undergone peer review

The Library of Congress Cataloging-in-Publication Data is available online at http://catalog.loc.gov

Typeface for the Latin, Greek, and Cyrillic scripts: "Brill". See and download: brill.com/brill-typeface.

ISBN 978-90-04-46155-0 (paperback)
ISBN 978-90-04-46156-7 (hardback)
ISBN 978-90-04-46157-4 (e-book)

Contents

Foreword

Twenty-five years ago, when I began the research that became *Use or Ornament?* (1997), there was little interest in the social impact of participatory art amongst funders and less in the elite art world. This innovative field of art practice, which had emerged in the 1960s under the banner of community art (and has since acquired a collage of labels, like a redirected parcel in search of an owner), was trapped in a policy paradox. It did not meet (or aspire to meet) the artistic standards of an art world whose authority it challenged and which reacted by damning community art as third-rate work by unsuccessful artists. But to consider community art's social value was equally unacceptable to an establishment that still believed in the illusion of art for art's sake. In refusing to align its products with dominant artistic norms, while prioritising the social dimension of its processes, community art found itself dismissed as mere artistic social work. Thirty years old, it had still to establish the terms on which it could be understood and assessed in the context of cultural and social policy, to say nothing of art, history or philosophy.

In the early 1990s, academia showed no interest in resolving this impasse, at least in the English-speaking world, though there had been work on theories of cultural democracy in France, and a boom in university research into cultural policy and management was not far off. In the face of general indifference, it was community artists themselves – notably Su Braden and Owen Kelly – who did most to develop thinking about the practice in the 1970s and 1980s. A decade later, it was the work of an Australian community art worker that showed me what might be possible in researching its social impact. *Creating Social Capital*, Deidre Williams' study of 89 Australian community art projects was published in 1995 by the Community Arts Network of South Australia. I contacted Deidre, in the days of the steam internet, and she subsequently wrote a working paper for my study. Her pioneering work had a large influence on my thinking and deserves to be remembered in Australia today.

After the publication of *Use or Ornament?*, I hoped that debates about whether participatory art produced social outcomes would evolve into consideration of the nature of those outcomes and their relationship to the conditions and processes involved. What mattered was not if there were social impacts, which seemed to me inevitable and undeniable, but what they were (always recognising that they were not only or necessarily positive) and how they were associated with the specific actions of community artists. That hope now seems naïve. The argument about whether participatory art has social value endures because it is political and because how it is resolved will have far-reaching consequences not only for arts funding, but for the whole field of social policy too. The original struggle between community artists and the arts establishment has, in the past two decades, moved into academia and policy circles where it thrives, equally acerbic and unfruitful.

That is why this book is so welcome and so valuable. Peter Wright and Barry Down have sought to move on from whether participatory art has social value to ask what it actually does, how that affects the people involved and above all how the two are connected. It matters because these questions can deepen artists' understanding of their work and so contribute to its development and improvement. I work often with young artists, people coming into a field that has grown enormously since the 1990s, and I listen to them asking the old questions about the relative importance of process and product, about quality, authorship, ownership and audiences, about intentions, relationship and the morality of social action, about funding and, always now, about evaluation. In the following pages, they will not find answers to those questions, which are contingent and give the work its restless dynamic, but they will find the materials with which to think better about them. And that is as it should be because community art – or participatory art, as it is termed here – is not, has never been, one thing. There is no 'correct' way to practice it, any more than there is a correct way to paint or make music. There are as many truthful ways to make community art as there are community artists, though not all of them have found or are even looking for the truth they are capable.

Scott Rankin is one who has, and he has drawn around him many others, including some whose stories are told here, building in the process a network more than an organisation, and a body of work that stands as a defiant challenge to that same art establishment that still maintains that high quality art can only be created by people it has accredited using methods it has approved. More than anything, Big *h*ART's truth grows from a refusal to lower its expectations – of itself, of the art it creates, of its audiences and, always, of the people it invites to make art together. Precisely because they are among those of whom much of Australian society expects nothing, Big *h*ART expects everything, and in doing so empowers them to prove to anyone who cares to see exactly what they are capable of achieving, for themselves, for each other, for their community.

In giving close, thoughtful and theoretically informed attention to the processes used by Big *h*ART's professional and non-professional artists, Peter Wright and Barry Down have produced a deeply instructive book about participatory art, and one that anyone concerned with this work will benefit from and enjoy reading. They have added to the small and precious body of texts that consider participatory art in terms of its own values, intentions and practices, rather than those others wish to impose upon it. This is one of those rare books that, as I finished it, I set aside to read again in a few months' time: it will remain close at hand.

François Matarasso
Morvan, December 2020

Acknowledgements

Books like this evolve in interesting and serendipitous ways. Borrowing from Grumet (2004) 'no one learns [or writes] alone' and we wish to acknowledge those who have contributed to the realisation of this process reflected in this volume. We stand, for example, on the shoulders of many fine scholars, artists and community workers both past and present committed to creating a socially just world. We endeavour to add to this broader social movement by engaging with and learning from a diverse range of people, places and cultures across regional and remote parts of Australia. Our purpose is to better understand the ways in which the performance arts can make a difference in the lives of young people and their communities.

We learned most from the lives of those young people who shared so generously of their time, knowledge and experience. We are indebted to them for showing us a spirit of curiosity, courage and optimism in the face of obstacles and barriers in their young lives. Their personal stories provide the inspiration and foundations of this book.

We extend a special thanks to Scott Rankin, Co-founder, CEO and Creative Director of Big hART Australia. Scott's ongoing passion and commitment to the performance arts and social change is truly remarkable. Scott's contribution in Chapter 2 provides an eloquent account of the philosophical, historical and political context of the work of Big hART in Australia and the broader role of the performing arts in society.

We were very fortunate to work alongside a number of valued colleagues on the original research team among them Brad Haseman and Michael White. During this phase of fieldwork we were also ably supported by wonderful research assistants at different times including Susan Thurow and Christina Davies, those participants and communities who gave gifts of time and experience often heart-felt and profound, other scholars and investigators including Dave Palmer, Diana James, and John Culley, and then Big hART workers themselves who all made various contributions in order that we might understand this work better. Further, we are grateful to François Matarasso who wrote the thoughtful Foreword; his contributions to the field and the pluralistic ways they have informed this work are significant.

We also thank Murdoch University for providing us with the space and resources to undertake this important work, and the support of the Australian Research Council. Finally, we would like to express our deep appreciation to our families, friends and life partners, without you none of this would be possible. We thank you all.

The research upon which this book is based was supported by the Australian Government through the Australian Research Council's *Linkage Projects* funding scheme (project LP110100619). The views expressed herein are those of the authors and are not necessarily those of the Australian Government or Australian Research Council.

About the Authors

Barry Down
is Professor of Education at Murdoch University, Perth Western Australia and Adjunct Professor, University of South Australia. His research focuses on young people's lives in the context of shifts in the global economy, class, poverty and dis/re/engagement in education. His most recent books include *Rethinking School-to-Work Transitions: Young People Have Something to Say* (Springer, 2018, with John Smyth and Janean Robinson) and *The Sage Handbook of Critical Pedagogies* (Sage, 2020, co-edited with Shirley Steinberg).

François Matarasso
is a writer, researcher and consultant with 25 years' experience in community-based arts development. He specialises in practice-led research, especially on the impact of culture, and in organisational support across the cultural sector. He has worked for international agencies, national and local governments, foundations and cultural organisations in some 30 countries. His work has been widely published and translated.

Scott Rankin
has directed the nationally renowned community development and arts company Big *h*ART for 25 years. He is a leader and teacher in the field of social and cultural innovation. Scott's reputation is built on a quarter of a century of work creating, funding and directing large scale projects in isolated, diverse communities with high needs. Scott is currently delivering projects nationally across Australia, as well as developing international projects. These site-specific, long-term projects tackle complex and multi-layered, seemingly intractable problems. Big *h*ART's award winning projects begin at the grassroots, assisting individuals, developing communities, driving change with policy-makers, creating art for flagship festivals, and sharing knowledge across sectors.

Peter R. Wright
is an Associate Professor of Arts Education and Research Methods at Murdoch University in Perth, Western Australia. He works across the Arts with a commitment to personal, social and cultural inquiry, agency, education and expression, health and wellbeing, and Creative Youth Development. His award-winning research includes teaching, learning and healing in, through, and with the Arts and what it might mean to 'flourish'. His research projects have received funding through the National Youth Affairs Research Scheme, the Australian

Research Council, Healthway, and Creative Education Partnerships Artist in Residence Scheme. Central to this work is learning and creative pedagogies, Teaching Artistry, ArtsHealth, social justice and inclusion, and the ways they are mediated in and through the Arts.

CHAPTER 1

Introduction

1   Why This Book, and Why Now?

Growing levels of inequality, social exclusion and lack of diversity and participation are defining moral challenges of our time made more pressing by the seismic shifts in the global economy that have ruptured the social fabric and connectedness of society. These issues play out daily in the political, cultural and media spaces and not only reflect precarious times, but also influence perceptions, shape the development and enactment of policies, and highlight forms of insecurity, displacement, alienation, conflict and degradation. As a consequence, social justice in the forms of recognition, representation and redistribution (Fraser et al., 2004) become pivotal, that is, who gets to be seen and heard, which stories are told, by whom and in whose interests. This matters, as in Said's words 'nations are narrations [where] the power to narrate, or to block other narratives from forming and emerging, is very important to culture' (1993, p. xiii). This means that the stories that are told or remain invisible are important in not only knowing who we are, and where we come from, but also whom we might become.

This book and the research on which it is based is located in the context of these 'uncertain times' (Macrine, 2009) where pervasive large-scale and profound social changes are wrought by global capitalism, and where narratives of dispossession (Harvey, 2003), vulnerability (Bauman, 2002), uncertainty and risk prevail (Beadle, Holdsworth, & Wyn, 2010). Whilst these broader forces may seem overwhelming, we believe participatory arts, with its emphasis on creativity, imagination and agency as the cornerstones of working with community, in community and for community, offer one powerful way of engaging young people in processes of individual and social transformation.

As we endeavour to understand how these processes operate we draw on the cultural work of Big *h*ART in Australia to help us illuminate the emancipatory potential of participatory arts in rebuilding young lives and communities. Big *h*ART has been a pre-eminent Australian example of participatory arts over the 28 years since its humble beginnings. Looking carefully at Big *h*ART's work, it is possible to observe creative ways of addressing the challenges of geography and place in rural and remote locations, escalating youth employment, tensions in relation to class, race and gender, the impact of globalisation and economic restructuring, and poverty. Each of these contribute to multiple layers of disadvantage for some of the most vulnerable and marginalised young

© KONINKLIJKE BRILL NV, LEIDEN, 2021 | DOI: 10.1163/9789004461574_001

people in Australian society. Indeed, the young people whose stories inform this book are what Bauman (2004) refers to as the 'wasted lives' or 'collateral causalities' (Bauman, 2011) of an increasingly callous economic system.

In these precarious times there is also a significant focus by governments, agencies and institutions on myopically mitigating risk rather than leveraging promise (National Academies of Sciences, Engineering and Medicine, 2019). This reductionist risk-adverse approach is a barrier to taking equity, inclusion and social justice seriously, addressing structural barriers to inequality including housing, health, employment and education, and identifying and encouraging creative opportunities to flourish.

Global international reports speak with status and authority, but sadly are rarely matched by a grounded practice that embodies the paradigm shift they call for. For instance, the Global Education Futures Initiative, drawn together from global organisations including the OECD, UNESCO, World Bank, ILO and WorldSkills, with 500 global education leaders from 50 countries, have produced a report entitled *Educational ecosystems for societal transformation* (Luksha, Cubista, Laszlo, Popovich, & Ninenko, 2018) in order to answer three driving questions in relation to skills, pathways and support for young people: (1) What skills and knowledge will help children, adults and seniors to lead fulfilling and thriving lives? (2) What learning models can serve individuals and communities in their learning journeys throughout their whole lives? And (3) How can educational systems support human flourishing and be an avenue for social transformation based on the values of compassion, humanity, justice and respect for the biosphere (or ecosystem) (Luksha et al., 2018, p. viii)? Ironically, the report also notes that the educational systems with 'the greatest potential impact on the future' are the most resistant to change because of 'taken for granted ideas from the past' (Senge, 2018, p. v). This observation points to the urgent need not only to challenge the status quo but to imagine alternative possibilities.

In response, this book traces the lives of marginalised young people involved in Big *h*ART – a not-for-profit cultural organisation – to help us better comprehend how these global dynamics are played out in the lives of young people. Based on their experiences, we attempt to identify what kinds of cultural, pedagogical and community-related conditions need to be brought into existence to enhance their life chances.

2   Key Organising Ideas and Purposes

In this context, the book is animated by four key organising ideas and purposes. The first is the possibility of *reinvigorating communities* through: developing assets and strengths, building community capacity and civic engagement, coming to critical engagement, and fostering a spirit of belongingness and connectedness. Second is *reinventing youth identities* through: interrupting deficit thinking, creating sustaining relational spaces, promoting health and wellbeing, considering alternative ways to promote rewarding and satisfying non-welfare dependant lives, and investigating youth and popular culture. The third is *reimagining alternative futures* through: identifying possibilities, pursuing the common good, developing an expressive and fulfilling life, and fostering creative, authentic and rewarding work. And the fourth is *fostering activist and socially just research* through: listening to young people, developing research approaches that are inclusive and respectful of the lives of the most marginalised, reconceptualising what 'counts' as evidence, equipping young people with research skills, and constructing and foregrounding narrative portraits of young lives.

In order to inquire more deeply into these four dimensions of social change, we turn our attention away from those formal institutional spaces like schools which have excluded far too many young people and instead investigate the informal and nonformal places and spaces[1] where organisations such as Big *h*ART endeavour to re-engage and transform lives through arts-based practices. These less formal spaces are increasingly important, as formal institutions of learning are not sufficiently nimble footed to respond to the rapid pace of social change nor the needs, desires, dreams and aspirations of young people themselves.

In supporting young people and communities to think anew and respond in more creative, democratic and activist ways in uncertain times, this book provides an opportunity to rethink theoretically and practically how we engage young people in participatory arts practice for social change. Big *h*ART, a dynamic and creative arts organisation, provides one powerful model of effective learning and community renewal based in the arts and grounded in these new global realities.

3   Big *h*ART

Big *h*ART, Australia's pre-eminent arts for social change organisation, has been at the forefront of participatory arts practice with marginalised and disenfranchised communities since 1992. Grounded in the maxim 'It is harder to hurt someone if you know their story', Big *h*ART works in challenging rural and remote areas, as well as impoverished urban contexts, to make the invisible visible, seeking to drive change in areas such as homelessness, domestic violence, slavery at sea, addiction and injustice.

What is consistent across each project described in this book is the characteristic of disadvantage, including for example young people at risk of self-harm, those who go through the juvenile justice system, and those who are marginalised and disenfranchised from mainstream contemporary culture and social institutions. In these 'precarious publics' there is 'a considerable gap between voice and influence' (Jenkins, Shresthova, Gamber-Thompson, Kligler-Vilenchik, & Zimmerman, 2016, p. 157). Drawing on participatory or socially engaged arts, Big *h*ART draws together the arts and the creative practices that are its DNA, promoting learning as a force for change, and responding to health and wellbeing inequities that flow from imbalances across physical, mental and social spheres (Marmot, 2014; Stuckey & Nobel, 2010) in order to build a more just, equitable and healthier society.

More specifically, and in response to the harsh new realities of economic instability, ecological damage, social inequality and human suffering, Big *h*ART provides participants and young people in particular with multiple ways of knowing, acting and being in order to engage in productive and self-fulfilling lives (White, 2009; Wright et al., 2016). Key to this practice, and consistent across participatory arts, is the way in which the arts activate and develop critical and creative capabilities through cultural learning – where there is active engagement in the creation of the arts and heritage (Cultural Learning Alliance, 2011). This engagement in cultural learning is complex, interconnected, empathetic and multiple in order to address not only what *is*, but to envision a different horizon by considering what is not yet, or what *could be* (Greene, 2005).

This imaginative capacity, strengthened through a social-aesthetic frame, enables young people to go beyond actions that reproduce objectivist, reductive, technicist and mechanistic ways of being and doing, to *think, act* and *be as if* things could be otherwise (Greene, 1995; Wright, 2017). Young people then potentially become imbued with a spirit of critical hope or, in Greene's (2005) words, a 'possibility of awakening' in order to overcome the damaging effects of the context in which they are forced to live. This spirit of hope reflects the 'cultural justice' that Rankin refers to in Chapter 2 as pivotal in order to thrive in contemporary times (see also Rankin, 2018). Arts participation, then, is rich in potentiality in the ways that it can be meaningful to the self, be future orientated, and contribute to the world beyond an individual (Malin, 2015).

In seeking to better understand these cultural processes, we point to the key principles that underscore these possibilities, and the ways of working, productive conditions and practices that animate them. In order to do this, we first point to some key themes that help contextualise our work and reveal how an 'economy of regard' (Offer, 2011) – lying between the market and a gift – helps to engage young people through acts of consideration, compassion, care and reciprocity. In this way, young people, and the arts-based processes Big *h*ART employs, are revealed as part of the 'hidden wealth' of nations (Halpern, 2010).

4 What Are the Key Themes Animating This Book?

There are a number of key ideas, themes and modalities that inform Big *h*ART's work including social-aesthetic learning, critical pedagogy, social and cultural justice, participatory arts and arts in health. Each of these are characterised by generative possibilities, the hope for what is not yet, the imaginative and creative capabilities enabled through arts practice and the social imaginary, and the learning always present through different ways of knowing, doing and being. The confluence of these possibilities is transformation. Transformation, and the consequential change in ways of being, lies in awareness, agency, and the social and cultural processes that can be both disciplining as well as eman-cipatory, and a space of contestation and resistance. The arts are locations of social and aesthetic production and practices that are 'complex, often contra-dictory, sites of social reproduction and ... potential sites of social transforma-tion' (Mahon, 2000, p. 467).

Each of these key concepts reflect theoretical and philosophical traditions that Big *h*ART animates through arts practice, cultural learning and the co-production of knowledge. This matters because, following Rankin, identity, that is, who we are and who we might be, is forged on the 'anvil of consciousness', and cultural power as an animating force comes from 'freedom of expression and research' (2018, p. 6). We briefly turn to each of these ideas in order to foreground the foundations upon which effective practice is grounded.

4.1 *Hope*

The building of alternatives is always a hopeful and educational act (Freire, 2014; hooks, 2003; Zournazi, 2002), and in order to better understand and make visible this process we note that Big *h*ART employs a pedagogy of hope – that is, new ways of knowing in order to enrich lives anywhere where ideas can be exchanged. Big *h*ART takes risks in order to achieve this, and transforms power relationships as both a process and product of its arts-based work. Reflecting the link between criticality and creativity, Freire (2014, 2016), bell hooks (2003), and Darder (2011) point to the ways in which the arts are an embodiment of public pedagogy, providing a space for humanistic inquiry, exploration and expression.

This means that learning – about oneself, others, and the broader sets of relationships that both enable and constrain – is always present. Part of this learning, Darder notes, lies in the criticality inherent in such approaches and the possibility of speaking 'truth to power' (2011, p. 799). In this sense Big *h*ART provides a 'place of seeing' or openness to change, embodying a humanising rather than dehumanising approach to its work, thereby providing visibility to and endowing dignity upon participants through learning.

4.2   *Transformation*

Big *h*ART's potential to transform its participants, that is, to create a different way of being, lies in the way it is informed by both an ethics of caring (Gordon, Benner, & Noddings, 1996), and the generative possibilities of culture both as *process* and *product*. Through cultural learning young people have access to the knowledges contained in a multiplicity of heritages, as well as contributing to what is not, but yet might be (Greene, 1977, 2003). By foregrounding the relational, moral and ethical elements of caring grounded in 'receptivity, relatedness, and responsiveness' (Noddings, 1984, p. 2), Big *h*ART works effectively with those who are disenfranchised from participation in culture by creating culture that is informed by and sensitive to people, place and context, rather than culture that is disembodied, dislocated and decontextualised. In other words, in employing an ethics of care, Big *h*ART works with people who are often invisible, and hence vulnerable (Rankin, 2014), towards *freedom to*, rather than *freedom from*.[2] Put differently, strengthening agency and cultural capabilities provides opportunities for cultural learning in order to move beyond the constraints inherently present when cultural life is dominated by commodities and restricted opportunities for a more hopeful life (Bowring, 2015).

4.3   *Capabilities*

Moving beyond the 'treatment' approach of early youth development work, where the focus was on what needs 'fixing' in young people, more critical approaches to youth development and studies have evolved (Ibrahim & Steinberg, 2014; Rios, 2011). These approaches draw on and extend what is sometimes referred to as 'positive youth development' (Catalano, Berglund, Ryan, Lonczack, & Hawkins, 2004; Silbereisen & Lerner, 2007) and 'creative youth development' (Montgomery, 2014; Stevenson, 2014). In these perspectives young people are seen as being *at promise* rather than *at risk*, recognising the generative possibilities of imagination, critical learning and life skills. This 'assets-based' rather than 'deficit' approach is reflected in Big *h*ART's work where young people's creativity is animated, focused and strengthened by engaging them as artists. By engaging in creative processes, they become makers and responders to issues that concern and impact on them.

This developmental process is circumscribed both by the technical and arts-based skills taught – often by highly accomplished artists and cultural workers – as well as the creative opportunities presented. These capabilities and associated processes of inquiry that are enabled through arts practices are then expressed, strengthened and shared. Tragically, and as one manifestation of a neoliberal ideology at work, this expressive capacity is often measured, quantified and starved of oxygen through traditional forms of schooling and education.

Growing out of the work of Sen (1992, 1999), where human development is seen as a 'freedom', and further amplified through the work of Nussbaum (2003, 2011) are the principles of belonging, mastery, independence and generosity (Brendtro & du Toit, 2005). This approach includes a holistic, people-centred concept of the ability to thrive, in which people have both the opportunity and ability to achieve outcomes that are both personal and social.

We were able to see each of these informing principles in both the cultural processes and the products of Big hART's work. We understand these capabilities to be innate in all of the participants (Dissanayake, 1995, 2000) that Big hART connects through its projects. More specifically, realising these connections between the arts, creative industries and everyday creativity can 'radically increase everyone's substantive freedom to co-create versions of culture' through what Wilson, Gross, and Bull (2017) refer to as 'cultural capability'.[3] In understanding these socially embedded freedoms, Big hART promotes a capabilities approach where co-creation includes the exercise and sustained use of the imagination, senses and capacities for thought (Nussbaum, 2011, pp. 33–34) – the confluence of which addresses the relational and emotional dimensions of disadvantage, or the blight of disconnectedness and corrosive 'social poverty' that exists in contemporary times (Halpern-Meekin, 2019).

4.4   *Cultural Learning*

The ways in which people engage with, learn and are shaped by context, including language, heritage and the forms used to represent them, are often referred to as cultural learning. In this understanding cultural learning involves both learning through, learning about and having access to culture (Cultural Learning Alliance, 2017). Important in this approach is that this form of active learning is participatory in nature and potentially a form of transformative praxis (Ledwith & Springett, 2010) where expression is used to act collectively in order to achieve a meaningful social goal. Arendt notes, for example, that positive freedom can only unfold though 'participation in public affairs, or admission to the public realm' (1990, p. 33). Our analysis of Big hART in this volume reveals that their work, based in cultural learning and cultural justice, facilitates this entrée and participation. Cultural justice is what guarantees the 'right to thrive' (Rankin, 2018) and it is achieved through socially and aesthetically mediated experiences. In this way, Big hART advances those who are marginalised or disenfranchised through culturally responsive methods that help mitigate societal inequalities.

4.5   *Creative Learning*

Creative learning focuses and further refines the notion of cultural learning in that it adds a methodology for learning about and learning for culture. This possibility of learning through and with arts experiences is grounded in the writings of John Dewey and notions of learning by doing and art as experience (Dewey, 1934/1959; Granger, 2006), Maxine Greene (1995) and the power of the imagination and creativity, the relational aesthetics of Nicolas Bourriaud (2002) where the social intersects with aesthetics, and the education of feeling and expression (Langer, 1952). Importantly, Matarasso (2019) notes that these organising ideas are always future oriented, and that each of these threads are brought together through participatory arts and cultural democracy. Interestingly, a 'trialogical approach to learning', where emphasis is not singularly placed on an individual or a community, but the collaborative development of shared artefacts (or objects), foregrounds the learning that occurs through the processes used to create and develop them (Karlgren, Paavola, & Beatrice Ligorio, 2020). This broader understanding is a powerful way to understand the learning inherent in these creative approaches. Linking these last two organising ideas, it is helpful to note the ways in which creative and cultural learning are analogous because they share certain axioms such as diversity, equality, inclusiveness and engagement. Creative and cultural learning through partnerships contributes to culture, with potential benefits for individuals, society and the nation at large.

4.6   *Cultural Justice*

Moving beyond traditional forms of cultural capital valued by dominant elites, which are potentially exclusive rather than inclusive (Bourdieu, 1986), Big *h*ART recognises and values other forms of knowledges that enable active participation in society. These forms of knowledge are not constrained by class, gender or other forms of affiliation and ways of belonging. This process recognises the plurality and inclusiveness of cultural literacies, and consequently 'cultural justice' (Rankin, 2018). Big *h*ART's work therefore embodies Roerich's observation that 'Culture belongs to no one man, group, nation or era. It is the mutual property of all mankind and the heritage of generations. It is the constructive creation of human endeavour' (2010, p. 48).[4] Through the preservation of diverse cultural values and heritage, culture and the ways in which it is storied have the capacity to 'transcend all obstacles, prejudices and intolerances' (2010, p. 48), a work no less relevant today.

4.7   *Arts and Wellbeing*

The field of arts and health is emergent, and arts and health research and theorising is 'diffuse and fragmented', drawing from a range of academic disciplines and creative agencies (Stickley & Clift, 2017). Thus to understand the potential of participatory arts, researchers draw on theoretical and conceptual tools from the cognate fields of health, the arts and learning theory in order to make visible how change occurs, what change might be, and the consequences of these (Clift & Camic, 2016; Kilroy, Garner, Parkinson, Kagan, & Senior, 2008; Stickley & Clift, 2017).

Big *h*ART, for example, particularly works with issues of identity, belonging and inclusiveness, and the social determinants of health,[5] working towards what has been broadly conceptualised as 'creative health' (All-Party Parliamentary Group on Arts, Health and Wellbeing, 2017). These conceptual organisers point to a more holistic understanding of what constitutes a healthy body, mind and community. This is played out through arts practices, and the consequent promotion of engagement and active participation in community, mitigation of social isolation, promotion of cohesion and diversity, and positive health and wellbeing benefits.

4.8   *Creative Praxis*

The unique characteristics of the arts, and the conditions developed and creative practices employed by Big *h*ART, make the production of different, more hopeful, knowledges possible. That is, there is always the possibility of learning – or openness to change – in the creative, generative and relational practices that are attributes of the arts themselves. In this social-aesthetic frame an educational power lies in the hopeful ways that pedagogy and the arts co-constitute each other. First, they are both social, for example, in Gallagher's words: 'pedagogy is what happens when people seek to produce knowledge together' (2002, p. xvi). In other words, individual agency is intersubjectively connected to others. Second, what the arts offer, and Big *h*ART embodies, are the opportunities for making that agency go beyond the simple (and important) transmission of critical knowledge, offering the development of critical creative capabilities that collaboratively and imaginatively revision the future through a praxis that is aesthetic, affective, critical, intellectual and reflexive.

The potential benefits of these developments can then be seen in the diversity of fields, domains, disciplines and theories briefly pointed to here including the sociological, physical, cultural, psychological and economic. This volume then helps build a framework for productive forms of practice, revealing some key philosophical and theoretical foundations upon which it is built. It also points to those domains of practice where change is possible, and the essential elements of those practices that animate collective creativity.

In a like manner, it is not our intent simply to claim an instrumentalist view or infer a series of causal relationships. We have seen too many 'turf wars' where questions of evidence or technicist approaches have actually done little to advance the field, but rather have served to further entrench defensive positions and have expended a lot of intellectual and emotional energy without furthering understanding or action. In a field that is inherently creative, and one that works towards creative outcomes, a plurality of approaches, languages, theories and concepts helps mitigate against such essentialist and reductionist notions, and enables us to better inquire into the complex relationalities at work.

As we continue to explore, think deeply and engage with this creative field of endeavour – one rich with promise as well as challenges and full of 'ambiguities' – we are also mindful of Matarasso's (2019, p. 197) call for more conceptual and theoretical work to help guide better forms of critique, focus and scale. This volume contributes to this particular scholarly and practical effort.

In this particular contribution we also, however, acknowledge the limitations of the written text that doesn't allow us to showcase the richly layered and multi-textual art produced by young people in the various projects described in this book. This would require a different kind of 'publication' or platform, one more suited to representing the multi-modal artistic productions (e.g., film, radio, plays, stories, music, jewellery making and so on) that were produced as a consequence of participation and engagement. To gain a better sense of the art itself, we encourage readers to explore the Big *h*ART website[6] where past and current productions are readily available and showcased.

5   Case Studies

The second level of context within which this book sits is elaborated through three case studies. In these case studies or studies of research sites, the key themes and driving principles of Big *h*ART's work are investigated and described. These three case study sites are: LUCKY, in North West Tasmania – Australia's island state; GOLD in the Murray-Darling Basin, a river system covering a large inland areas of four states (Queensland, New South Wales, Victoria and South Australia) and Australia's 'food bowl'; and NGAPARTJI NGAPARTJI, a project based in Alice Springs (Northern Territory) and the APY Lands[7] of Australia's desert heart. In LUCKY, Big *h*ART worked with young people to build community and to address crime, self-harm, ageism, exclusion, social isolation and dislocation. The GOLD project involved working with rural and farming families under extreme stress as a result of the 'Big Dry', Australia's worst recorded drought (Pincock, 2008), giving a human face to climate change and changing water use practices, including suicide prevention.

The last case study, NGAPARTJI NGAPARTJI ('I give you something, you give me something'), was conjointly developed with Indigenous Australians based in Alice Springs in central Australia. This project drew on the lands and language groups of the Western Desert – Australia's largest cultural block. The key aims of this project included the preservation of language and cultural knowledge, and sustained positive change in struggling Indigenous communities.

What was consistent across all of these projects was the ways in which the arts were utilised to create a platform for creative participation and engagement for the participant communities in order to forge a sense of cohesion and purpose in the participants' own daily lives. For example, we consistently observed the ways in which individuals and communities who may otherwise be unheard and silent created a presence for themselves by articulating their concerns and issues through a process of collective critique and introspection. In so doing, they shaped their respective social and cultural spaces. In addition, each project was multilayered, utilising a range of art forms and processes, and also intergenerational.

6   What Kind of Research Informs This Book?

The research that informs this book occurred over a prolonged interest in Big hART's work and then an intensive three-year period involving a team of researchers from three different Australian universities and one in the UK. This intensive period of research followed the form of multi-site ethnographies (Burawoy, 1991; Marcus, 1998), where observations, semi-structured interviews and various forms of documentation, media texts and performances were analysed. Part of this process involved participant observation of workshop processes and the not-yet-articulated tacit knowledge of practitioners' (arts workers') everyday practices (Polanyi, 1966). These embodied knowledges helped reveal a great deal about what otherwise might have remained hidden.

These processes of inquiry provided methodologies that were sensitive to practices, context and voice, rather than just outcomes. In this way we drew on the practice-based knowledge generation that has been part of Big hART's development. There were four specific participant groups involved in the interview process: first, the young people and community members who were directly involved in workshops, performances and installations; these were the participants who created and contributed to the creative works produced – the 'participatory' element of participatory arts. The second group were the arts workers and creative producers who ran workshops and facilitated engagement and participation, that is, those who enabled the work. The third group were the broader communities surrounding the participants, including in some cases a national audience for the screening of documentaries, a national touring performance, and associated arts festivals. And finally there were the funders, that is, those who supported the projects through financial and in-kind assistance. Each of these four groups provided overlapping and revealing perspectives on both the process and products of these projects, bringing different sets of values and expectations.

Building on the narrative impulse that is a key tenet of this practice, we also employ narrative portraits (Lawrence-Lightfoot, 2005; Lawrence-Lightfoot & Hoffman Davis, 1997) in order to help humanise the key outcomes of the work. These portraits were developed from interviews with participants and serve to give voice to the participants, thereby helping to contextualise diverse participants and their experiences. In addition, thematic analyses of interview data, researcher journals and fieldnotes (Miles, Huberman, & Saldaña, 2014; Saldaña, 2016) were conducted.

7   How This Book Is Organised

Considering these two iterative contexts, that is the 'big picture' and then drilling down to the sites of application, this book is organised in the following way. First, following this introduction that describes 'Why this book, and why now?', we provide an overview of the way that Big hART has developed including its philosophy, history and pedagogy. This chapter, drawn from the original research report, presents in a poetic way Scott Rankin's story of Big hART revealing its values, aspirations, processes, and informing principles.

The following six chapters take a series of key concepts – relationships, self-efficacy and agency, expressive and meaningful life, good work and citizenship, capabilities, and 'becoming somebody'– and explore them in the context of participants' stories and the cultural pedagogies that enable them. These portraits of participants' lived experiences, where each identifies with a marginalised or disadvantaged group, provide a rich context for revealing the challenges and potential benefits of working with such precarious publics. This takes what is 'local' and experiential and links these with a broader network of ideas that then become tools for sense making and interpretation.

Finally, we draw these threads together and look at how we may better understand the work of Big hART, recognising that all such work is contingent, always imperfect, contested and emergent. In the words of Freire (2007) this kind of transformational work is underpinned by a 'pedagogy of the unfinished' which recognises the complexity, fragility and struggles of cultural workers and educators. Importantly, Freire's notion of 'daring to dream' reminds us that our purpose is to move beyond the fatalism of the circumstances in which we find ourselves. In pursuing this task, we deliberately seek out the productive possibilities by describing '*where* it can, *how* it can, *with whom* it can, [and] *when* it can 'be accomplished' (Freire, 2007, p. 64). We do not wish to down play the barriers and interferences to social change nor present an overly romanticised version of reality. Rather our intention is to capture those 'pockets of hope' (de los Reyes & Gozemba, 2001) which are both instructive and hopeful in terms of making a difference in the lives of marginalised young people and communities.

Based on our fieldwork we describe the seven domains where change and transformation occur: enhancing health and wellbeing through networks and relationships; building communities through creative spaces; developing agency and a sense of efficacy; using participatory arts for an expressive life; constructing productive lives: aspirations and work of value and meaning; strengthening capacities and dispositions for learning; and (re)inventing identity through cultural practices.

Next, in seeking to better understand the question of 'in what ways?', we synthesise and foreground 20 'productive' conditions and practices that are enablers of change, recognising that these are multiple, and necessary but not sufficient in and of themselves. Key to understanding the roles that these productive conditions play are the caveats that they are always contingent, dynamic, in tension and culturally bound. What these do, however, is point to the value of 'local theorising' (Risjord, 2019) as an important context for debates and learning to occur. They remind us that we can usefully be informed by the particular as well as the global, and that our knowledge is particularly powerful when grounded in lived experiences.

Notes

1   UNESCO supports the importance of different spaces, places and pathways for enhancing access to learning in all parts of the world, going beyond formal institutions such as schools and colleges (http://uil.unesco.org/).

2   *Freedom to* (Berlin, 1969), relates to making choices, being self-determining, having self-mastery, acting or *positive* freedom. Negative freedom, by way of contrast, is *freedom from*, such as being free from interference – a view espoused by neoliberalism. In negative freedom impediments to choice might be removed; however, being free to work means little if there are no jobs. Positive freedom means that there are not only opportunities, but also the capacity to take advantage of them; this relates not only to individuals but also socially determined groups – refugees, youth, First Nations people, or other marginalised or disenfranchised groups.

3   Cultural capability is understood to be the combined freedom to speak, to express, to be heard, to experience, to make, to build, to contest, and to create (Wilson et al., 2017, p. 5).

4   Nicholas Roerich was a Russian activist and painter whose work led to the Roerich Pact, a pact that has influenced international law standards, UNESCO protocols, and public activity protecting cultural values and heritage (Barenboim & Sidiqi, 2010).

5   The social determinants of health (as defined by the World Health Organization) are the conditions in which people are born, grow, live, work and age. These circumstances are shaped by the distribution of money, power and resources at global, national and local levels. The social determinants of health are mostly responsible for health inequities – the unfair and avoidable differences in health status seen within and between countries (WHO, 2020).

6   See https://www.bighart.org/

7   The APY Lands are a distinctive region comprised of three Indigenous language groups of the central desert: Anangu, Pitjantjatjara and Yankunytjatjara.

CHAPTER 2

Big *h*ART: Origins, Foundations and Making a Difference

Scott Rankin

1 Beginnings

Big *h*ART sprang to life almost by accident in 1992 in the small industrial town of Burnie on the northwest coast of Tasmania – a town made infamous by Midnight Oil's song of despair 'Burnie':

> ... two children in the harbour,
> they play their games storm water drains,
> write their contract in the sand it'll be grey for life ...

In 1992, with an arts career progressing well, and having maintained an ongoing commitment to social justice, my gaze and that of a producer friend (John Bakes) shifted towards the possibility of applying the process of making art in acute and targeted ways to particular issues. The issues we had in mind were presenting in the community with some urgency, yet seemed invisible in the media and politically. Our discussions led us to think about the privileges for the creative person of living an expressive life, and the many positive and entwined layers to this creativity: the sense of being able to take action, agency, understanding, response and affirmation, and sometimes power; the way in which the arts can illuminate stories that are not visible in the general community; that communities and individuals could be invited into constructing new kinds of narrative, which could be fed into the narration that describes the future and becomes the nation, and so on. These were all very grandiose claims, but we were younger and addicted to the possible.

These ideas seemed especially outlandish when I looked at what was then being called 'community art' and noticed how much of the art made under this label seemed deeply compromised by mediocrity and was something of a haven for broken artists as much as for broken people participating in a project. It was dispiriting. There were of course passionately argued reasons why work made through community processes – though poor in quality – had to be critiqued in a different, more conciliatory way, how these stories belonged

© KONINKLIJKE BRILL NV, LEIDEN, 2021 | DOI: 10.1163/9789004461574_002

to others beyond the artist and how the process was what really mattered. It seemed to me, however, that the most obvious thing was that the artists were failing the community groups they were working with, bringing an intransigent and blocked creative practice to new settings. We were our own worst enemy: jaded, hard-working artists, renaming poor work as brilliant. The more practised and better-funded areas of the arts looked on with condescending smirks at our efforts.

Yet there were unique and important skills being honed in the community cultural development disciplines: new mentoring skills, empathetic skills, authenticity and flexibility, applied art techniques, community diplomacy and much more. It seemed to contain potential new languages beyond the jaded offerings and creative slurry pouring wastefully from mainstream practice. A fresh commitment to virtuosity was needed in this difficult area, using new pallets and disciplines. What seemed promising was a return to a deeper practice, more centred in the whole of life, away from models of art making based on commodity, manufacturing and tourism.

It seemed abundantly clear to us that this community arts practice was frequently encountering communities with very serious survival issues and a very low skills base. Attempts were being made to achieve very big goals for multiple stakeholders, with tiny amounts of funding and very little infrastructure. The arts disciplines that needed to be exercised were intensely difficult. They still required the thousands of hours of practice, but also required a deep pool of inter- and intra-personal skills to work in contexts where these issues were clear.

The timeframes for these projects would also need to be long and would be expensive, yet the pool of funding was always so limited, and the end product difficult to sell (the funding was deliberately structured this way by state and federal bodies). Making art in these contexts was an endeavour that needed brilliant producers, and yet – in this era– there were no producers being trained in the sector. The notion was not even thought of (now of course anyone with a spreadsheet is a producer apparently). It was like a practice built on a foundation of good hearts, the promise of optimism, the smell of an oily rag and the desire to save. Failure was built in, structured, from a policy level down.

Artists working in communities felt and behaved defensively. People were so burnt out and struggling with such important issues that any criticism fell on deaf ears. Ranks closed. There was little interest in change or professional development; people had their heads down just trying to survive. What made it even more difficult was that this intense and taxing creative discipline and the resulting practice was hardly even recognised as more than a sheltered workshop for artists who could not cut it in the mainstream. Larger arts companies would sometimes dip in and out, if there seemed to be a buck or some funding kudos in it, ignoring the discipline of community process, like blind giants dancing.

It was in this context, after ten years of trying, that in 1992 the Big *h*ART model was born. It was an attempt to wrestle with the many layers of the practice, to experiment with the dramaturgies of work in community, and to approach this work with a longing for virtuosity. What was needed was an approach that would signal the significance of this cultural work, and show the consequences of this to the funding stakeholders. Then we could gain access to many different areas of society and reach a broader audience. We could also move beyond being pigeonholed as the arts or, worse still, community arts, of which deep down we were immensely proud.

The Big *h*ART experiment was a recognition that unique benefits could be found in both the process of making and the experience of consuming the story. If the process was deep and the artistry strong, the work could be made with such finesse and authenticity that a shift, an illumination, an understanding could be created in key places: portfolios, electorates, media and opinion formers, for example. New hidden stories could be released into the narratives around which individuals, communities and the nation formed. These early experiments gave us the opportunity to define different layers that each Big *h*ART project would need to work on, and different approaches that would need to be kept in play, like spinning plates in the air.

2   The First Projects

Our very first project happened almost by accident. We were invited to work on a prevention project for young offenders – which was going badly and would have lost its remaining funding – in a regional town on the north-west coast of Tasmania. At the beginning of the project youth workers and police reported one offence per week from the fifteen young people in the target group. At the conclusion of the project, they recorded only one offence in 10 months.

Although not yet officially named Big *h*ART, and not yet an incorporated body, the company quickly gained attention through the success of its workshop approach to stemming recidivism amongst this young target group. Participants were engaged enough to deliver creative products in the community. The project attracted independent evaluation – unusual at the time. This 'outside' independent observation proved useful, and this process soon became part of the Big *h*ART model.

Interestingly, many participants from this initial project have stayed in contact over the years. They have ended up contributing to the community in a variety of ways, from raising children to managing tourism operations, joining the armed forces, working in aged care facilities and so on. The following are two portraits drawn from this first project. For the purposes of this book, the participants' names have been changed.

2.1   *Portraits from the First Project*

Nat was a young woman who was feared by the police for her physical strength and capacity for violence (she was the only woman to escape from Risdon Prison). Nat had been essentially locked indoors away from interaction with the public for much of her childhood, and abused both sexually and physically. The family suffered from intergenerational obesity and mental illness. Nat became central to the arts project and to the life of the group. She toured a number of performance pieces with the company, spoke at public functions and went on to employment. Some years later she rang to say hello late one night from an aged care facility where she was working. 'Guess what?', she said, 'They've left me in charge of the drugs cabinet!' At the time of the project, this would have been inconceivable, as the future being predicted for her was framed by failure and perceived danger to the community.

Cynthia was agoraphobic, obese, highly intelligent, socially isolated and bearded. This young woman had every reason to feel rejected and angry. She initially began coming to the workshops after the other participants had left to help with the cleaning up. After a few weeks, Cynthia started arriving while the workshops were in progress. She would cope by sitting under a table and watching. It became clear that she enjoyed confined spaces and, as it turned out, although large, she was extremely flexible. This socially isolated young woman ended up having the main speaking part in a large touring experimental stage production. She would begin the show inside a seemingly small road case, which would burst open later during the show and she would roll out. This confined space seemed to give her confidence and calm her nerves. She went on to contribute in many valuable ways to the community.

There were many others, such as Jim, the almost illiterate son of a local detective, who arrested him before the project, and I could go on. Most of the group involved had a story of disengagement and disadvantage, and this came out in numerous, often violent or attention-seeking ways. One of the first workshops for the group involved an exercise on the stage of the local theatre. In the centre was a large stack of china crockery from the local second-hand shops. As the workshop progressed, under the glare of the theatre lights, participants were asked to come forward and break a plate in front of the others. In this context, this extroverted group, known for their vandalism after dark around town, were desperately timid.

Little by little, however, they began to understand the power of this 'staged space', where the transgressive and the flamboyant could meet, where audacity was an asset, where the public demanded controlled shows of violent energy ... and so the plates were flung over and over cathartically at the back wall, shattering across the stage in an occupational health and safety nightmare. Their potential and inclination towards anarchic creative energy was both broken open and harnessed. Two of the shows we made together – GIRL and Pandora Slams the Lid – went on to tour and win awards. Tragically, while the company was on tour with two of its works to the National Festival of Australian Theatre, an ambulance officer in Burnie was murdered by the peer group of this young cast. Had they been at home it is likely they would have been at the same gathering. It proved a salient counterpoint to the contribution to the broader community these young people were making.

3   Million-Dollar Kids

Young people such as these could be called million-dollar kids. From the time they first come to the attention of various government departments – at around two years of age – to the time they are spat out of the system at 18 years, they have a million dollars or more spent on their wellbeing. These costs to the system include wages, administration, infrastructure, interventions, repair to premises and occupational health and safety. The system that is supposed to support these young people is often of little avail, and two decades later the situation is usually much the same, except the figure is far higher. (For example, one young person close to a Big *h*ART project costs the state 500,000 dollars a year and this will continue for many years to come.)

On the strength of these initial projects and their evaluation, Big *h*ART began searching for other opportunities and was able to secure substantial non-arts funding to pilot and document further strategies. The skills of arts workers were utilised on targeted projects which responded to related issues in the community such as domestic violence prevention; HIV/AIDS prevention amongst rural young people who were injecting drug users; re-engagement with school; and teenage mothers in transient relationships and their vulnerable children.

Each of these projects attracted government attention through independent evaluation and consistent use of the media, resulting in increased funding opportunities and growth. This rapid growth and attention required Big *h*ART to formalise its internal company structure, find a permanent name, and document its purposes and processes.

The company was fortunate in its naivety. There was no formal committee, no status could come from supporting it, and so we were something of a cleanskin. There is far more pressure now for new organisations to resist the entrepreneurial spirit and follow the textbook versions of organisational structure, governance and risk mitigation. Even in 1996 the push had begun towards a sausage machine mentality for small start-ups like Big *h*ART – imposing a one size fits all, manufacturing approach to management structure in community and arts organisations.

However, Big *h*ART was fortunate at the time to meet a very elderly semi-retired local lawyer who offered to do the work pro bono. The beautifully Dickensian Mr Crisp was skinny, with a leathery face and enormous cabbage ears, and was deaf as a post. Suited in double breast and navy pinstripe, a simple swish of his thin silver hair was enough to send a cloud of dandruff wafting across the room. Mr Crisp yelled with the rasping whisper of a man who knew his gasps were numbered. But he was free and, as it turned out, wise. He said he would do the legal work for us on three conditions: our board would be as small as possible, it would meet as infrequently as was legal and our constitution would be minimal. Big *h*ART finalised its constitution and incorporation early in 1996, along the lines Mr Crisp required, and we have been grateful ever since.

4   **Gaining Prime Ministerial Support: Martin Bryant and
       John Howard**

1996 was a watershed year. The conservative government was new and in April the world looked on in horror as gunman Martin Bryant went on a sense-less killing spree in Port Arthur in the south of Tasmania. The link between Tasmania and violence became lodged in the national consciousness.

A number of the young people involved in Big *h*ART projects were not dis-similar to Martin Bryant: socially isolated, numb, disconnected from education and hurt. There was a clear sense that if they had access to weapons similar tragedy was possible. Having worked with this group for a number of years, having written up the approaches we were using, and having been evaluated, we were in a unique position to approach the newly elected Prime Minister John Howard MP. The Prime Minister was looking to reach out to Tasmania to try to show strong leadership on the issue of guns and violence – so he was receptive to a positive story of community-driven change.

Perhaps in a first for a small not-for-profit arts organisation, we had found an Australian Public Service mentor who was deeply interested in change and able to guide our approaches to Canberra. We had already decided we wanted to have a bigger impact than just in the local community and, for this goal, we had to try to have input at a policy level. With her guidance we hired what really amounted to a lobbyist to work on our behalf. Our lobbyist approached the Department of the Prime Minister and Cabinet regarding the Prime Minister meeting some young Tasmanians who were no longer connected to the justice system, but instead were contributing positively to their community.

Prime Minister Howard also agreed to launch Big *h*ART, our newly incorporated body, and a manual capturing our approach at Parliament House, Canberra. The Prime Minister entered the theatrette in a flurry followed by the media scrum. I remember my partner Rebecca was holding our young son Lockie, who was chewing a rusk. The PM stopped momentarily on seeing a baby and Lock offered him a chew of his teething biscuit (astute, as Mr Howard in the first weeks of government had a few teething problems of his own). In the theatrette the PM commented on the confidence of these young people, noting their disadvantaged background and their courage in breaking away from their likely social trajectories.

It was only really in the months and years following that we realised the value of having the imprimatur of the incumbent Prime Minister associated with Big *h*ART. Being able to say 'launched by Prime Minister John Howard' proved invaluable in opening doors, triggering us to think more strategically about access to government, contribution to policy change, and new approaches to cross-portfolio funding. It helped us avoid a backwater of irrelevance in the safety of the arts and instead to produce projects of scale that punched above their weight and were aimed at multiple audiences.

What developed out of these practices was a model of working at the grassroots; utilising hybrid cultural approaches and non-welfare strategies; working with the local community's strengths; taking the work produced into the public domain through arts festivals and the media; and then targeting the policy domain beyond the arts. The key findings from these projects were then used to bring about more sustained change and information sharing in policy and research contexts.

This was still at a time when little evaluation was done and research on the ground with these kinds of projects was almost unheard of – an arts project was pigeonholed and relegated to a bread and circuses cliché. In breaking out of that mould, Big *h*ART stumbled on an approach for future endeavours that is still being refined today. Interestingly, in breaking out of that mould, we also avoided the gaze of the sleepy, self-satisfied dinosaur that is 'the arts'. Gazing admiringly at their own adorable little metro-centric navel, they literally did not know we were around for ten or more years, and this is the best thing that could have happened. Instead of approaching the kitchen, plate in hand, grateful for a small dollop of funding gruel, we were in the back lane, raiding the mini skip for piles of leftover funding from all kinds of departments (tipped off by our lobbyist). Big *h*ART was so lucky to be the bastard child of a hidden affair between structural inequity and arts myopia in the Australia Council.

5   What's in a Name: Capturing the Essence of Big *h*ART

The silent 'h' of *h*ART became a way of symbolising our intention to keep the 'heart' implicit in the values of the company. In other words, we were unashamedly attempting to make a difference through our work; however this change was based in the long-term processes we used in communities through projects that resulted in art being made.

Furthermore, this silent 'h' can be found in the participatory processes used, the advocacy work with policy, the values used in the workshop processes and the company itself, in the work with the community as well as in the viewer's experience of authenticity in the art being made. It also alludes to the company's intention to try to make work of consequence, tied to communities with high needs where change is essential, rather than just making work without a selection criteria. To this degree there was 'heart' in the political nature of the projects and the urgency of the issues being dealt with. The name captures the company's approach across different domains, such as in the arts, in policy discussions, and in cultural solutions within communities.

The 'Big' component of the company's name is not so much about scale, but rather its consequence. It reflects the company's interest in contributing to society and bringing creativity to the centre of life, the whole of life, rather than relegating it to the realm of hobby, diversion or commodity.

When people say 'Big Heart' it also alludes to 'the heart of the country' and the iconic place it holds in our collective consciousness, and how there is more we can be taught by the land itself and the First Peoples of this country. When we began twenty years ago, the name resonated with our interest in focusing on rural, regional, remote and isolated communities. It hinted at what we have not yet been taught by the country we live in as we huddle by the coast, waiting for boats to arrive to take us home to somewhere.

The company name has also always been somewhat enigmatic. We do not dictate how people pronounce it, whether it is said Big Art, with a silent 'h', or Big Heart. This proved more and more useful as the company gained recognition across government departments. Departments whose focus was social or community oriented tended to warm to the notion of the 'Big Heart'. The arts sector and audiences would usually pronounce the name 'Big Art'. This helped us avoid preconceptions that could pigeonhole our work and gave us useful access to diverse circles; this ambiguity allowed us to diversify our funding sources, without many rivals.

Lastly, 'big' also resonates with 'big ideas' and captures the size of the issues that Big *h*ART is tackling and the scope of the company's attempts to work strategically on projects of scale. And it is 'big' in the sense of the consequences we can expect from placing art differently out in the world. Linking 'Big' with '*h*ART' is the powerful work of story.

6   The Role of Story

If we regard our lives as being lived 'in the moment', with a past that no longer exists and a future that is not yet real, it is useful to think of our 'nation' as an ephemeral thing, as a series of 'narrations'. It is a set of ideas wrapped up in a story that comes from the past, and is written in the present as a way of establishing definitions of what the imagined future may be. There are dominant stories; stories that no longer have currency; stories that are not really that big or important but are growing in stature (think Gallipoli); stories that are deliberately excluded (e.g. the way we dishonour our elderly and let them languish in unseemly and dispiriting nursing homes because we are too scared to face our own mortality); and stories that are invisible.

Propaganda utilises many of these tools; however art does not lend itself to propaganda because the inward journey, the contemplative journey, the journey of depth tends to expose the propagandist to the audience, rather than trick the audience. Art tends to move away from the static and the impulse to 'conserve', to keep things as they are. The poetic impulse collectively meanders its way towards the sublime, and into the new. This is not a linear progression forward; rather, it is a spiral inward, in tension, deepening, not in single generations alone, but across time and generations. These notions help us understand the way that story is employed by Big *h*ART.

6.1   *A Person's Story Can Be Their Last Remaining Valuable Asset*

In any community, those who have been excluded, whether deliberately or accidently, are often on the bottom rung of the community. Their invisibility has economic consequences. Often their very last asset is their story. It is often valuable, because it acts like a canary in the coalmine. If told in the right way, and placed with the right audiences, these stories can illuminate things we need to know about ourselves and things we need to shift as a society. In other words, these stories have high value and act like 'gifted consultants' who can help shift society by their input into our ideas about ourselves and our social policies that can change society for the future.

The discussion of these unfolding stories in all forms through song, dance, science, theology, media and sport, each with different entry points, are what we often call culture. It is the very essence of each of our waking hours. Whether we are the kind of person who contemplates it or not, we are all involved in this story making. The litmus test of the health of this discussion is empathy.

Empathy is different to sympathy. It comes from the Greek *empatheia* (*en* – in and *pathos* – feeling). Empathy is deep, involving entering into the life of another. Sympathy is from the Greek *sympatheia* (*syn* – together with and *pathos* – feeling). Sympathy is not so deep. It is still valuable, but it is experienced alongside, in contrast to empathy which involves entering into the experience. This empathetic response can end invisibility and provide protection for those in the community who have found themselves excluded from the narrative.

6.2   *Story as a Protective Mechanism*
One of the basic principles of Big *h*ART's work is that a person's story can act as a protective mechanism, or a restraint on the clumsy damage that society can inflict on some groups through a lack of understanding. If young people know more of the story of older people in a small country town, the older people will feel an increased sense of safety. Most people are very tolerant and supportive of their neighbours when there is shared story or circumstance – this is often experienced in times of natural disaster, when people are involved in a common 'story' and have a common set of tasks to achieve.

6.3   *Creating Broader Audiences*
The more pressing the issue, the deeper the invisibility, or the more a story is being manipulated by others, the more critical it is for the stories to be broadly and deeply seen, heard or experienced beyond theatre and arts circles. Ideas are still valuable in small circles for triggering new iterations of thinking; however, change comes through a groundswell, not the chop whipped up on the surface by the wind. The process of change can be supercharged by knowing the different audiences for your work, using the media, involving decision makers and softening key hearts, and this comes from being strategic in thinking and in disseminating the story.

This role can be defined as 'social impact', and 'social impact producers' are attracting philanthropic attention and funding. Their job is to ensure the work is reaching nodes in multilayered networks that spark further change. This may mean broader general public audiences, but it also means targeted audiences who can respond to a growing groundswell with shifts in the national story and then shifts in policy.

When authentic high-value stories, created in collaboration with gifted artists, are illuminated well and placed in 'high-value' forums – such as arts festivals – the response is profound, and appreciation cathartically expressed. These stories are 'expressions of self', and one of the strong foundations of Big *h*ART's work is returning an audience's appreciation of this 'self-expression' to those who are experiencing the issues, and who have expressed it through their story. This in turn can create intense moments for the participants that trigger strong new self-appraisal and often require new choices about who they are in the face of the issues they have experienced; their new-found visibility; a sense of now being included and having a worthwhile contribution to make. If this process is mentored, these participants in BIG *h*ART projects will often begin to make different choices about changing their social trajectory. This is not some therapeutic magic pill, but rather a natural consequence. It is harnessing one of those moments in life when we instinctively have permission to re-evaluate our identity. This re-evaluation, in turn, gets expressed in choices we make in our social trajectory. Finally, because Big *h*ART is interested in social and individual change, these moments are then supported and mentored, and as individuals make new choices pathways are created on Big *h*ART projects to open up new possibilities.

CHAPTER 3

Relationships, Place and Wellbeing: Do I Matter? Where Do I Fit In?

> **Story**: As a young mum you can feel alone and isolated, looking for help, especially those mums who have always been at home. It's a place you could go and socialise that didn't cost us anything. (Kylie)

Kylie' story reveals a great deal about the importance of relationships, place and wellbeing in young people's lives. She participated in the LUCKY project, where she gained experience in working with young people to build relational spaces in which young people could forge friendships, pursue passions and interests, and contribute in socially worthwhile ways. Kylie lives in Tasmania. She is in her twenties and is a mother of three. Kylie started off as a Big *h*ART participant, but as the project evolved and her confidence grew she went on to help the project team with recruitment, project tasks, cleaning and child care. Kylie provides a unique perspective into the impact of a Big *h*ART project as both a participant and then subsequently as a project worker. She was able to talk about changes she experienced as well as changes she observed in others:

Connecting and sharing our stories

> It was great for socialising for them who didn't get out. It was great for the kids … we made friends. There was a real thing about connecting and sharing our stories. We did jewellery making. I still make jewellery now. I make all my own. The project let parents know that there is things out there for them. They can have opportunities even though they have kids. Like we did our Tourism Certificate through that. Everyone got a certificate so now you can be the guide on tour buses and things like that with that qualification. It gave them a qualification and just knowing that you can do something.
>
> One of the people that has really changed is Michelle. She now does a full-time course at TAFE to do aged care. She's doing her second year of that. This is someone who didn't do anything, who has never done anything in her life at all. It's [the project] got her out there and doing something. I think my public speaking improved 'cause I always got dobbed in to do the speaking. Now I work in a call centre and have to talk

© KONINKLIJKE BRILL NV, LEIDEN, 2021 | DOI: 10.1163/9789004461574_003

to people even more. I do tech support for computers. Which can be fun. We do Apple computers and I had never used one before so it was four weeks training and exams every week.

As a young mum you can feel alone and isolated, looking for help, especially those mums who have always been at home. It's a place you could go and socialise that didn't cost us anything. Sewing as well. I know Kim now sews flat out. We did a big sewing thing. Kim made a blanket for her son that she was really proud of. The hard thing with Kim is that she has never been good at anything and everyone has always put her down for it. But now she knows she can do stuff, which is just a big confidence builder as well. The difference for her was the fact that someone was willing to give her a go and to help her to try to do it. Kim had changed so much. Her confidence is heaps better. She is willing to get out there and try to do stuff and not let anyone tell her that she can't. Knowing there are people that care about her and are willing to give her a go and help her has been the biggest thing for her. She's trying to get her driver's license at the moment. She is continuing to try.

We did a thing where we shared recipes, like on the LUCKY website where you could do it from home or you could use the computer there. For This is Living we interviewed the older people in the community for background stories and things like that. To go up to strangers and talk to them was a massive thing for some people. I did a lot of the typing up of the interviews and listening to them and typing them up was amazing, listening to the stories ... We thought we had it bad but it was nowhere near as bad as the stories that I heard. Jewellery, sewing, writing, expressing our feelings through the writing, and not being afraid to express ourselves and have other people see it. Mostly through Facebook a lot of us still communicate heaps. Making new friends was important. We keep up to date with what each other is doing, what's going on, things like that. The key thing is social connections for those who don't reach out, to have been involved in something where they have had that chance to reach out and know there are people there who are going to listen and not judge what they are saying.

1   Introduction

In this chapter we explore Kylie's story to explain the centrality of relationships, place and wellbeing as key ingredients in the performance work of Big hART. Drawing on Kylie's experience, we consider why relationships matter in terms of confidence, self-worth, pride, identity, hope and wellbeing. We also gain an insight into the ways in which participants benefit through enhanced feelings of happiness, enjoyment, excitement, acceptance and empowerment. We then move on to identify the productive practices that need to be created and more widely sustained to enhance the relational dimension of communities. These practices include dialogue, listening, peer support, caring, activity, social networks, choices and access to community 'funds of knowledge' (Gonzalez, Moll, & Amanti, 2006) in order to build a spirit of inclusiveness and respect in which relationships can flourish.

The focus is on understanding what it means to be in relation within the context of Big hART artist productions. We want to understand how young people from adverse backgrounds and circumstances become mentally healthy through self-expression, perspective (the comparison of self to others and therefore seeing things differently), self-determination (the option to choose what they would like to do rather than being told), and building a sense of efficacy, confidence, positive self-image, resilience and belonging.

Of interest is the unique manner in which Big hART is able to work with participants, artists, funders and the community to enhance the wellbeing of people involved in its projects. Also of significance is the way Big hART projects show participants there are possibilities available to them by strengthening their capabilities and capacities (see Chapter 7). In the process, Big hART helps participants to feel more secure by creating friendly and safe places to work, with people who care about them deeply, who do not judge and will help participants succeed.

Through projects such as LUCKY, NGAPARTJI NGAPARTJI and GOLD, many participants described how they moved from feeling isolated to being connected with their communities by expanding their network of friends and acquaintances, creating positive peer relationships, interacting with artist and community mentors, participating more fully in their community and 'escaping' their everyday lives. According to participants, Big hART had an affirmative impact on their life by increasing their sense of confidence, self-esteem/self-worth, self-image/self-pride, hope for the future and enthusiasm.

Whilst the centrality of relationships cannot be underestimated in these transformational endeavours, it is much harder to describe and explain the actual theoretical and practical processes involved. In this task, Sellar (2012) draws on Deleuze and Guattari to provide us with some clues by deploying the idea of friendship to help explain how 'joyous encounters' and 'intellectual hospitality' can foster the affective conditions in which new knowledge is produced about the self and our worlds.

Working alongside teachers in 'disadvantaged' schools in South Australia, Sellar (2012) attempts to unsettle simplistic explanations of relationships, and instead advances a deeper philosophical and pedagogical understanding of the ways in which relationships are talked about and enacted. He explains: 'friendship conceived as a joyous encounter between compatible bodies and ideas, as a form of intellectual hospitality, implicates certain of our affective connections with others in movements of thought and learning' (2012, p. 72). This 'affective turn' in educational research allows us to open up new lines of inquiry by asking some different sorts of questions to help us think differently about human potential and possibility 'or the conditions of emergent becoming' (Robinson & Kutner, 2018, p. 116).

Sellar (2009) goes on to explain how pedagogy is 'an inherently relational, emergent, and non-linear process that is unpredictable and therefore unknowable in advance' (p. 351). Stories like Kylie's enable us to better understand the processes of sense making, whereby 'once the pedagogical event has unfolded, and participants are afforded sufficient distance to reflect on and narrate what has occurred, it should become knowable' (p. 351).

These important theoretical contributions enable us to appreciate the relevance of stories of young people like Kylie in far more creative, complex and sophisticated ways. In doing so, we can begin to see the centrality of relationships in creating the productive conditions for thought and action.

2   Productive Practices

We now move on to consider how this affective turn opens the way for creative thinking and learning through the production of high-quality artistic performances. Based on the experiences of participants, we can begin to extrapolate a set of relational conditions that foster, for participants, alternative ways of being in the world.

2.1   *Drawing on Community Assets, Leadership and Resources*
Each of the Big *h*ART projects described in this book sought to develop community assets, leadership and resources through the shared experiences of making art. The emphasis was on building local capabilities by increasing the wellbeing of individuals, especially those most marginalised from their communities. For example, we were often able to observe young people like Kylie who initially came to projects as participants, then went on to contribute to new project iterations and to provide support borne from their experience

of project engagement and participation. In a like manner, local assets were mobilised through participants having a voice, and speaking their own words. This meant, for many participants, there was a greater sense of agency created in the context of being in relation with others and enabled through shared experiences of making.

Such views are hardly new. In *Sometimes a shining moment*, Eliot Wigginton (1986) describes the processes whereby he and his students forged a different kind of project-based pedagogy grounded in the lives of students. Researching the history of artisans and crafts of local people living in rural Appalachia, these student researchers investigated their community's historical lineage and published their findings in a magazine called *FoxFire*. This outlet provided young people with opportunities not only to connect to their local histories, assets and resources but to produce astonishing levels of engagement, adult responsibilities and academic skills (Margonis, 2004, p. 39). At the heart of Wigginton's work is the view that all learning occurs in the context of human relationships and this is best achieved by connecting people socially and intellectually to their communities (Margonis, 2004, p. 48).

Kylie described this kind of contextualised inquiry in This is Living, an arts-based community project in rural Tasmania. In her words,

> we interviewed the older people in the community for background stories and things like that. To go up to strangers and talk to them was a massive thing for some people. I did a lot of the typing up of the interviews and listening to them and typing them up was amazing, listening to the stories ... We thought we had it bad but it was nowhere near as bad as the stories that I heard.

Kylie's experience in This is Living reflects the principles and values of a wide range of community-engaged learning approaches including: students as researchers (Steinberg & Kincheloe, 1998); communities as curricula (Theobold & Curtiss, 2000); and place-based education (Gruenewald, 2003a). According to Gruenewald (2003a), these 'places *teach* us about how the world works and how our lives fit into the spaces we occupy. Further, places make us: As occupants of particular places with particular attributes, our identity and our possibilities are shaped' (p. 621).

2.2   *Reinventing Individual Identities*

Participation in Big *h*ART projects helped participants to understand and improve their own sense of identity and wellbeing. These 'free spaces', as Evans and Boyte (1986) describe them, provide opportunities for young people to 'sculpt real and imaginary corners for peace, solace, communion, personal and collective identity work' (Fine, Weiss, Centrie, & Roberts, 2000, p. 132) – or what Proweller (2000) refers to as the process of 're-writing/righting identities'. As Kylie explained:

> expressing our feelings through the writing, and not being afraid to express ourselves and have other people see it. Mostly through Facebook a lot of us still communicate heaps. Making new friends was important. We keep up to date with what each other is doing, what's going on, things like that.

It is well established that social inclusion impacts on one's sense of self and well-being (Vinson, 2009). Participants in LUCKY, GOLD and NGAPARTJI NGAPARTJI were able to individuate, discover new trajectories, and feel affirmed and recognised within their own communities, and more broadly, through media attention and strategic placements in public festivals and national television. In short, participants like Kylie understood that they mattered and, importantly, had something worthwhile to contribute in communion with others.

2.3 *Building Positive Relationships*

Big *h*ART seeks to fosters positive relationships within and between the participants and the community, therefore promoting values of trust, respect and care. This relational component of the work is key as relationships of trust allow participants both to be 'stretched' and grow, but also to be 'held' as they take risks in exploring new identities and possibilities. Kylie explained: 'It was great for socialising for [those] who didn't get out. It was great for the kids ... we made friends. There was a real thing about connecting and sharing our stories'. She went on to describe how 'As a young mum you can feel alone and isolated, looking for help, especially those mums who have always been at home. It's [Big *h*ART] a place you could go and socialise that didn't cost us anything'. Importantly, across each of the three sites examined in this book, learning about the self and world occurred most powerfully in the context of others.

In this context, Hutchinson's (2004) notion of a 'pedagogy for strangers' is helpful because it enables 'a different way to see each other as strangers' (p. 75) by moving 'toward a realization of a type of intimacy among strangers' through narrative (p. 79). The aim is to build what Judith Green describes as 'deep democracy' (1999), characterised by a spirit of interconnectedness and free communication with a commitment to 'reconstructing civic institutions, processes and expectations' (p. xiv). Creating democratic narrative relations of the kind advocated by Hutchinson (2004) involves a number of key tasks:

- Learn enough about each other without ironing out all the uniqueness of our differences and be comfortable with remaining strangers.
- Understand that strangers do not pose a threat to us individually or as a group.
- Be especially aware of the long-dominated cultures … we are a nation of immigrants.
- Recognize that we do share similar human needs across the many cultures in our society, but we must be sure that we unlock our heads and not expect every culture to express or meet those needs in the same way as we do. (pp. 87–88)

2.4   *Developing a Spirit of Inclusiveness and Respect*

Big *h*ART values each participant and encourages them to engage in artistic processes that enhance health, wellbeing and social justice. This means accepting that participants are still developing skills, knowledge and capabilities. To this end, Big *h*ART recognises that working together enables more to be achieved because no one is left behind. In addition, Big *h*ART accepts that each participant has a contribution to make and is respectful of individuals' rights and identities and the successive contributions they make towards high production standards. Fundamental to this capacity-building process is the notion of 'relational trust' (Bryk & Schneider, 2002) or those social exchanges which bring with them 'respect', 'personal regard for others', 'competence' and 'integrity' forged within a set of mutually interrelated dependencies (see Smyth, Down, & McInerney, 2010, p. 74). Kylie endeavoured to explain how this spirit of inclusiveness and respect plays out 'for those who don't reach out' by affording opportunities to be 'involved in something where they have had that chance to reach out and know there are people there who are going to listen and not judge what they are saying'. This attitude acknowledges the importance of avoiding judgements, accepting young people for who they are and offering a place where they are not alone.

2.5   *Nurturing Imagined Futures*

Finally, Kylie's story illustrates how young people can benefit from activities which appeal to affect. Kylie explained how artistic processes afford opportunities for participants to imagine their futures beyond what already exists. For example, Michelle, who was involved in the LUCKY project, developed an interest in aged care and enrolled in a TAFE course where she was in her second year. According to Kylie, 'This is someone who didn't do anything, who has never done anything in her life at all'. The LUCKY project 'got her out there and doing something' and thus created opportunities she had never previously imagined. For Kim, another participant in LUCKY, the opportunity to design and produce a blanket for her son played an important part in helping her to feel a sense of accomplishment and confidence as a parent. Kim was a single mum who felt like 'everyone put her down … but now she knows she can do stuff'. In this context, notions of relationality, friendship and hospitality are even more imperative in re-imagining young people's futures. As Kylie so ably pointed out, 'The difference for her [Kim] was the fact that someone was willing to give her a go and to help her to try to do it. Kim had changed so much. Her confidence is heaps better'.

3   Conclusion

Drawing on Kylie's story, this chapter has described a set of productive practices created by Big *h*ART projects for the purpose of engaging young people in creative projects, thereby providing support, knowledge, self-empowerment, hope and perspective as they create their imagined futures. In Kylie's words:

> The key thing is social connections for those who don't reach out to have been involved in something where they have had that chance to reach out and know there are people there who are going to listen and not judge what they are saying.

These projects provided the necessary spaces for participants to build relationships in a spirit of hospitality and friendship based on the values of respect, trust and care for each other. In this context, Kylie's story helps us to better comprehend the processes involved in this kind of relational activity and the subsequent opportunities to develop knowledge and skills (especially multi-literacy skills), reduce feelings of isolation and reinforce to participants that they matter.

CHAPTER 4

Agency, Self-Efficacy, and Social Transformation: 'Step by Step Changing My Life for the Better'

> **Story:** Really it has led to my job, where I am now. So it started with
> LUCKY ... just being taught, you know, to feel lucky about having children.
> They were making us feel important because we were mothers and that.
> And that's led to me being comfortable enough to go beyond that and to
> get the job that I've got now ... So I think that everything that I've done
> right from LUCKY through to DRIVE just led to where I am now.

Hilary, a young woman who came into a project, serves to illustrate how she
came to 'do things differently' in order to change her life for the better. While
Hilary's story illustrates agency and also a level of interconnectedness across
the domains of change we have identified, she was able not only to describe
her own experiences of agency and what this meant in terms of self-efficacy,
but also her observations of this development in others.

Step by step changing my life for the better

The early years of my life were troublesome. When I was 13 I abused alcohol and drugs and I surrounded myself with friends who reinforced this
abuse. I went to school until Year 11; when I was 16 I had my first child and
left. It wasn't until I was in my early twenties that Di [a Big *h*ART worker]
asked me to be a part of a Big *h*ART project, which she described to me as
a crime prevention program. At first I was reluctant to participate, but my
sister and me went together. In the beginning we would only go unless
we went together, but after a while we became confident enough to go on
our own. Over the years we have participated in LUCKY, Radio Holiday,
Drive and This is Living.

Being involved in these projects changed my life for the better. The
people at Big *h*ART supported me, they got down on my level, they
respected me, they never judged me, and they helped me confront my life
and my choices. These things started to affect me. I started to feel happy
about myself and lucky to have children. I started to feel important. I
questioned my comfort zone, like the kinds of friends I kept. Big *h*ART
gave me a new circle of friends who were on the straight and narrow – I

could disconnect from those other friends of mine. And this meant that slowly, step by step, I stopped doing the drugs. I haven't touched marijuana for 6 to 7 years now, and I haven't touched anything else, except alcohol, for 3 to 4 years. I'd say that these Big *h*ART projects got me started in changing my life for the better. I would never have thought we could do something like this on our own, but after a while these projects made us realise that we could go it alone.

And I know these projects have affected other people in a similar way. People who are or used to be involved are on the right track now – they have got jobs, they've got married and they've bought houses. Even I've bought a house now. I've learnt that anything's what you make it.

1   Introduction

In this chapter we examine the impact of participatory arts on the development of agency, self-efficacy, and social transformation through Hilary's story. We consider both what this might look like, and the enablers and constraints, highlighting the ways in which 'culture' can be either an 'emancipatory tool' (Holden, 2010, p. 3), a site for exclusion (UNESCO, 2019), and/or zone of 'contestation' and 'contact' (Ross, 2008; Somerville & Perkins, 2003). Bauman, for example, points to the way that culture can be a site for 'creativity, invention, self-critique, and self-transcendence' as well as a tool for imposing social order (1999, pp. XVI–XVII).

The notion of learning, with both these negative and positive implications, links the affordances and the constraints of these forms of experiences. We now turn to examining the implications and outcomes of these arts-based experiences that Big *h*ART facilitates.

Key to better understanding the role of Big *h*ART in an ecology that combines the arts, learning, health and wellbeing, and social change, is the way in which culture can be a repository of, and place for, learning. More specifically, arts practice and the layers of learning within it contain opportunities for learning new skills (Stern & Seifert, 2009), critical knowledges, self-confidence and respect, as well as different ways of being and not simply doing. In this understanding the potentiality for change lies in the ways that being agentic can animate both people and ideas, and the way that cultural learning is not only rooted in the past, but is also a process of creation. As Appadurai explains, 'it is in culture that ideas of the future, as much as those about the past, are embedded and nurtured' (2004, p. 59). In addition, the creative processes that Big *h*ART employs, and its participatory (and democratic) ways of working, ensure that 'the future does not belong only to the already privileged few' (Blyth, 2013, p. xi).

This observation points to the broader role of the arts in social change and the ways that this begins with participants. More specifically, the power of creativity, reflected in both process and product, has the potential to lead transformation through risk taking and the ability to see things as if they could be otherwise (Greene, 1995). In this way participants can move beyond ambivalence and what are often unstable lives.

2   Agency

Going beyond cultural learning as simply transmission, this broad domain relates to a person's sense of agency, in this case meaning being present and active in the world and acting upon the world. This includes action for the sake of ends or outcomes, rather than mere acts in and of themselves (Korsgaard, 2009). At its best, the notion of agency encompasses being confident and purposeful, learning in and through action (Bresler, 2004; Wright, 2011), and being an active constructor of meaning (Bruner, 1996). The notion of agency foregrounds individual choice, freedom and intentionality; it speaks to being purposeful and the benefits that flow including having and taking control in one's life (Hempel-Jorgensen, 2015).

This notion of agency can be understood by way of contrast to people who feel diminished and passive, have a lack of self-belief and self-respect that makes them vulnerable to abuse or manipulation, have the disempowering belief that they should 'give up', are powerless, lack control or feel they are not worthy. In other words, a lack of agency results in people feeling small, worthless and inadequate with no capacity to change or affect anything in their future; these feelings are described as 'learned helplessness' in psychological terms (Seligman, 1972) and they often arise through no fault of their own. Being purposeful, by way of contrast, is the 'intention to accomplish something that is both meaningful to the self and contributes to the world beyond the self' (Damon, Menon, & Bronk, 2003, p. 121). The arts provide engaging and meaningful opportunities for 'purposeful development' (Malin, 2015) that has meaning and value.

Key to understanding this domain is the fact that the psychological construct of 'learned helplessness' with its associated feelings of powerlessness, hopelessness and an inability to change is contingent, and goes beyond psychology into social action. In addition, while behavioural change can be thought of as individual, and based on logic and rational choice, this domain reveals that behavioural change grows out of Big *h*ART's practices of community, social acceptance and experiences borne of deep engagement in heartfelt dialogue, creative acts, expression and reflection. In this sense, agency is more than simply 'knowing' the facts or having critical knowledge, but is also relational and for participants reflects 'beings and doings' that have meaning and value. It is also important to understand that each of these beings and doings and what constitutes meaning and value are culturally circumscribed and culturally bound.

Through Big hART's projects, and the cultural solutions that they afford (Rankin, 2014), participants are able to be active and feel like they have agency. These feelings of agency build confidence and so lead to transfer into other aspects of participants' lives through the creative ability to write/re-write identity. Consequently, while motivation to change comes from within, it is wrong to think of individuals as silos; we are profoundly affected by the company of others and the feelings that are engendered, for example. Hence, it is possible to look at this domain for evidence of impact of participatory arts projects where participants move from limiting behaviours – either internally or externally imposed – to those that are self-enhancing and self-affirming through the creative acts that arts practice enables.

Simply put, a creative act is an act of agency rich with possibility that moves beyond directed or duplicated activity that reproduces what is taken as given. So while behavioural change, or doing something differently, is evidence of change, the process of change grows from feelings and the actions that flow from them. This fosters self-efficacy, in this case meaning the belief or confidence in one's ability to achieve a goal or task (Moorfield-Lang, 2010). This means that we might look for how someone does something differently as evidence of the impact of a Big hART project; this being one point on the continuum of change (Schaffer Bacon & Korza, 2010).

3   Attributes and Dimensions

Hilary's story reveals that agency grows over time, has a number of attributes, and is an outcome of the 'productive conditions' that were the enablers and the practices in which she engaged and participated in order for agency to be strengthened (discussed shortly). In considering these six attributes we are able to more clearly see the ways in which agency is strengthened in participatory arts projects.

3.1   *Agency Is Iterative and Develops over Time*
First, and unsurprisingly, agency as a capacity develops over time. It is not lockstep and does not have a trajectory that continues in a straight line. Instead,

it is relational and contingent, and aligns with a developing self-awareness, reflecting Dawson and Andriopoulos's (2017) observation that agency is both temporal and processual. Hilary described her experience of this process in this way:

> You observe it over time and because you're a part of it … part of the change, um, you … you've got to take a step back sometimes to see it … to actually see the progress you've made, because it's incremental and I … I see a … sort of a … more of a willingness for kids to buy into this [as a process] this time around.

3.2   *Providing Opportunities for Participation and Engagement*

Second, the strengthening of agency is highly contingent on providing opportunities for engagement and participation. Consistent with participatory arts, and reflected across all the projects we studied, this attribute points to the multiple entry points into a Big *h*ART project, including in this instance food, catering for and accepting difference, and underscoring the possibility of creative opportunities. Participants may also join a project through a friend, word of mouth, or as the project develops over time.

However, simply providing opportunities to participate where none may have previously existed is key. It is also important to understand that such opportunities for creative learning and expression can be precluded by restrictions such as geography (Anwar McHenry, 2009), class (Bourdieu, 1993; Holden, 2010), cost (Ware, 2014), or where programs are developed away from, and without consultation with, the community itself (Wright et al., 2016). Hilary talked about how she became involved in this way: '[My friend] Curtis dragged me around one day. I got free food, and you guys fed me so I just kept coming. It was just fun and it was always something different'. Hilary went on to explain the context:

> there is nothing for teenagers in this town at all. There is nothing for unusual teenagers in this town. You can be part of the … the cool kids and hang out with each other which is … or lap the street which is completely gay and boring. But this was different … not usual. You couldn't do this [creative] stuff at school or you sort of just had to come across it.

3.3   *Working as Artists*

A third, and critical, attribute of agency in this context is working as an artist. The project participants act as makers, and they can be seen progressively adopting and embodying this role. Working in this way provides for many a different way of being and acting in the world. By way of example, Hilary described the process of creating stop-motion movies[1] and another creative place-making process.[2] More specifically, she was asked to describe some of the ways she had been involved as a 'maker', and the creative processes she had been engaged with:

> When we do all those little things and shit; the stop-motion things ... time capture or whatever; where you take a picture of whatever they were called and interviews and photos, more photos, more photos. And then kind of went on like that for a while.

Hilary found pleasure in these creative activities and a creative place-making process of creating ephemeral art: 'And I liked them videos of when, like, you took [us] ... all to make that big eye in the middle of, like, nowhere which could be seen from space'.

3.4   *Developing Self-Awareness*

The fourth attribute, reflecting the iterative and integrative nature of these attributes, is developing self-awareness. Hilary described some aspects of herself and others in the project, noting the way in which they both viewed themselves and had been perceived in the community, and then some of the pathways used by Big hART in order to address these issues: 'Most of us have disabilities. One way or another we were all outcastes'. She continued: '[Big hART] used to get us to do these stupid little games; I suppose trust games and stuff because there is a lot of people aren't trusting, like me ... It helped'.

Recognising that learning is notoriously difficult to define, and that learning and change are linked – with learning either a precursor to change, or a result of change – we were able to observe that, fifth, learning is always implicit in arts practice (Wright et al., 2013), and can occur in a number of ways including learning a new skill or art form.

3.5   *Learning in and through Arts Practice*

This form of arts-based learning not only provides the tools for multi-modal inquiry and expression, but conjointly strengthens a participant's creative capabilities (Nussbaum, 2011). This foregrounds the role of experience, and the aesthetic nature of art as experience (Dewey, 1934/1959), reflecting what is felt, seen and done.

Showing an interest in and aptitude towards photography, Hilary referenced not only what she did and enjoyed, but some of the feedback she received as a consequence. More specifically she enjoyed: 'Photography, filming little stuff was kind of fun', and she described that she 'took heaps of photos [that I] remember. I went into that junkyard where we were all living at, and I took all those awesome photos and everyone thought they were really good'.

3.6   *Seeing Things Differently*

Sixth, as a consequence of having been provided opportunities, and supported to learn new things, Hilary was then able to see herself differently, feeling more purposeful and confident. Hilary now sees that she is able, that what she does makes a difference, and that she can plan for a future knowing that she has choice, can be intentional, and has confidence:

> [LUCKY] just gave me interests I didn't know I had. Future plans. I've sort of got my head on. So it was interesting. It probably just gave me options to go to the cities actually. That is about it which come in later. It is the one thing I probably really gained from it.

She added: 'I suppose I give things more of a go now than I would have'.

Taken together, this means that Big *h*ART creatively works with participants through first providing opportunity. Before anything else, Big *h*ART provides opportunities that would not otherwise exist; this is especially important where there are areas of low or non-existent cultural opportunities. In this case, Hilary's participation and then engagement deepened both over time and through different project phases. What Hilary did not describe here, but was recounted by arts workers, was that she developed from initially being a project participant, to acting as a mentor to other young mums in later project phases. So from being an initial recipient of support, Hilary then became a provider and mentor, revealing both the generative nature of the practice and also how benefits accrue incrementally and over time, and the ways in which reciprocity can be enabled.

Next, the ability to act on the world grows from social and physical support, in this case, from support provided by arts workers engaged on projects. Importantly, this support has a number of characteristics. In the first instance it is practical and ranges from providing transport to food. Second, a defining characteristic is that it is non-judgemental and treats project participants as equals with strengths and abilities, not with deficits that need to be remediated; this points to the highly relational nature of agency. In addition, agency can flow not only from learning *how* to do something, but from, thirdly, a confidence (self-efficacy or belief) that the doing will *count*, that is, what is created will be of value. In this way, and fourthly, acceptance, support and creating combine to build confidence and respect. Put simply, Big *h*ART's practices create a context where equality is not only an informing principle, but is purposefully enacted.

Finally, and linked with learning, is the way that skills are taught and developed. Agency, for example, is enabled by skill development. Sam, who participated in GOLD, recounted:

> What I've been like given from the project is personal things like communication skills ... before I started GOLD I was pretty isolated ... I didn't communicate properly, I had trouble working with people and one of the major things I got from Big hART was working with people not just on a physical level but at a creative level.

This young person highlighted that social and physical support reduces feelings of isolation, and then links with skill development to provide life-affirming choices. Hilary, for example, began to make what can be seen as better health and life-enhancing choices. It is also evident that the work is creative in the way that Sam mentioned, foregrounding particularly the interconnection between the arts, agency and self-efficacy.

In short, arts practices are both a source of agency, and agency at work. This can be understood when we think of how an artist is known by his or her creative act, giving form to feeling for example, and bringing something into being. Importantly, agency is also profoundly intertwined with participation, as agency influences the frequency and depth of participation, and participation increases agency.

A funder also identified agency in an interconnected way. He emphasised that he was struck by:

> [s]tories of individual young people who have gone on to do other things ... who have gained a huge amount of confidence from doing this kind of work and it's something that they found meaningful and purposeful so it is good for their personal development and it seems to have energised them around representing community and community issues.

Agency, then, results in and iteratively contributes to gains in motivation, an increase in the quantity and quality of social networks, the confidence to do other things, and feelings of hope, independence, achievement and empowerment. In this domain of change one can look for evidence of project impact through the reconfiguration of experience in terms of what is *see-able* and *say-able*. In short, the arts are a powerful route to agency and self- and social development with the potential for changes in socially ascribed status.

The following describes four productive conditions that were present in Big hART's practice that enabled agency to be developed. We recognise that these conditions are necessary but not sufficient for change to occur.

4   **Productive Conditions, Practices and Possibilities**

4.1   *Participation and Engagement through Art*
All of the projects we studied reflected the notions of acceptance and respect. Inclusion, for example, means that diversity is welcomed and results in feelings of connected belonging (hooks, 2009; Wright et al., 2013). Arts-based approaches offer multiple entry and exit points across contemporary, attractive and accessible ways of making and, while Big *h*ART's projects are highly processual, they are neither a matter of simply process or product, but rather each iteratively informing the other across modalities and forms. For example, poor quality art is not simply accepted as slippage because the participants are not professional or highly achieving artists. Instead, Big *h*ART's arts processes and practices result in the creation of high-quality artefacts, often through the mentorship of highly accomplished artists.

Furthermore, it is important to understand that, consistent with the other domains of change we describe, there are overlaps, consistencies and resonances across different levels of practice. In particular, agency and feelings of self-worth, respect and efficacy are enabled through art practices and the creative conditions that surround them. What this looked like was reflected in participants' engagement with and personal investment in arts processes and products that were both open-ended and built towards a (or in some cases several) high-quality artefact – performance, original music, photography, documentaries, digital stories and the like. These were strategically placed in international and national arts festivals, and promoted through free-to-air TV and radio, other media platforms, and high-profile public events such as those at Parliament House in Canberra and Federation Square in Melbourne.

These outcomes, both process and product, developing skills and knowledge in arts making and producing with others, shapes, shares and makes visible the cultural and creative wealth of communities through engagement, participation and pleasure. This supports social change through 'extending opportunities for those who have had least opportunity to engage, participate in and enjoy excellent arts and culture' through co-production (Evans & Piccini, 2017, p. 100). Meaning is not only made through making and production, but also through the audiences that 'read' the work (Radbourne, Glow, & Johanson, 2013).

4.2   *The Discipline of Public Performance Outcomes*
The open-ended creative processes Big *h*ART uses are then directed into successive iterations of rehearsal in order to have a public viewing of the work. This meant, for example, that participants have to be present physically, emotionally and psychologically in order for a quality performance to be realised. This

discipline is contingent on the quality of relationships formed, and feelings of ensemble and responsibility towards others. In addition, the way that culture is celebrated through performance means that heritage is animated, with participants being active cultural creators rather than being disengaged or passive receivers. More specifically, this leads to participants' feelings of being in, and belonging to, something bigger than themselves. Consistent with this discipline is mutuality and conjoint responsibility, in this sense, as one young person said, 'getting my eyes up' and seeing a broader horizon, learning that success is dependent on self- and shared responsibility.

4.3 *High-Status and Quality Mentors Providing Models and Support for Creative Action*

Each of the three projects employed various national and international artists who were 'available', supportive, skilful and accessible. For many participants being able to work with these professionals and see them 'at work' provided models of application, humility and status, and an entrée and insights into an arts world that was previously inaccessible. What participants often gained from this productive condition was an understanding of the working life of an arts professional, and in particular the commitment required over sustained periods of time, in often challenging working environments, in order to deliver high-quality outcomes. Participants also gained the pleasure of association, status gained, and support from faces they knew though media exposure.

4.4 *Learning in a Social-Aesthetic Space*

In this productive condition skills were taught in context and at a point of need. For example, a performance in a riverbed at night in a remote community meant that lighting and sound had to be effective, distractions dealt with and relationships built with audiences, all important skills learnt in context and at a point of need. At the other end of the scale oral histories had to be collected by participants from informants who often lived challenging lives. This meant that these key informants had to be engaged, respected, facilitated, and carefully listened and attended to. Each of these elements implied a certain level of sociality, and kinaesthetic or 'felt' responses that required both awareness and responsiveness.

In overview, and consistent with results of arts engagement described elsewhere (Davies, Knuiman, Wright, & Rosenberg, 2014; Davies, Pescud, Anwar McHenry, & Wright, 2016), evidence of change was visible in:
– confidence
– self-belief
– communication, particularly public speaking

- tolerance
- trust
- respect
- persistence.

5   Conclusion

Agency in a Western cultural context is often privileged and seen by some as a key developmental task for young people. What is often missed, however, is that agency is contingent on opportunity, learning, resources, culture and social equality – it is a journey rather than a point to be reached. We consistently observed that Big *h*ART was concerned with adolescen*TS*, that is, focusing on the individuals who participated, rather than adolescen*CE* as a broad homogenous group (Vagle, 2012). Big *h*ART employed the social imaginary to strengthen agency (Cocke, Rabkin, Williams, Haft, & Goldbard, 2007). This meant that difference became an asset rather than a deficit, thereby adding value to young people's lives though what they both lived and embodied. In this sense, Big *h*ART developed agency as capacity-in-action using the arts as both the process – pathways towards – and products of (through the high-quality artefacts created) this change.

As Hilary reflected, participants' self-beliefs also changed through these agentic processes. Bandura, a social-cognitive theorist, described this as having a sense of self-efficacy that is comprised of 'people's judgments of their capabilities to organise and execute courses of action required to attain designated types of performances' (1986, p. 391); in Big *h*ART's case this was linked to the opportunities to learn new skills, strengthen capabilities, and achieve tasks previously thought to be 'too hard' or beyond one's reach. This form of confidence or belief in one's self can flow from arts experiences into other areas of people's lives (Moorfield-Lang, 2010).

In a like manner, the benefits noticed by participants, arts workers and community members are more than mastery of a new skill or technique and include, as Hilary reflected, social-emotional benefits. This asset-based form of development is now being referred to as 'positive youth development' (Damon, 2004). Research also highlights the saliency of such arts-based approaches for those who are marginalised and traumatised (Development Services Group, 2016).

Sen's (1992) description of a people-centred 'capabilities approach' does much to help explain this form of developmental trajectory. More specifically, the development or change that informs Big *h*ART's approach can be thought of as a form of 'freedom' (Sen, 1999), that is, the freedoms people have to be able to live the valued lives to which they aspire. Nussbaum (2003, 2011) underscores the associated importance of creativity in human dignity and social justice.

This form of freedom is especially salient for those with whom Big *h*ART works, where people who are disadvantaged can be defined as 'those who are least able to realise their potential and develop and exercise their capabilities' (Adamson, 2010, p. 9), which occurs in a context of rising inequality (Adamson, 2010). This means that agency is not just individual, but also relational, and systems and government also play a role. What is key however, is that the capabilities whose attributes can develop through cultural participation are the capabilities that people need in order to lead the lives they want (Jones, 2010), thereby expanding the realm of human agency and freedom.

Finally, in the words of Schumacher: 'Development does not start with goods; it starts with people and their education, organisation, and discipline. Without these three, all resources remain latent, untapped, potential' (1973, p. 139). With people like Hilary, then, Big *h*ART 'step by step, makes my life better' through 'making something new', 'connecting deeply with others' and 'having a positive impact' [on them], and 'sharing something of myself' [with others].

Notes

1   Stop motion is an animation technique that involves physically manipulating an object that is then photographed in single frames. When the images are stitched together in a fast sequence, the illusion of movement is created. Stop motion is an effective learning tool when introducing movie creation by lessening the complexity of the learning curve.

2   Creative place-making is a process 'where partners shape the physical and social character of a neighbourhood, town, city, or region around arts and cultural activities' (Markusen & Gadwa, 2010, p. 3).

CHAPTER 5

Affective, Expressive and Meaningful Lives: Storytellers, Dancers, Performers

Story: I think NGAPARTI was really identity building for Ernabella; that community particularly and for the individual participants as well from wherever. Certainly I think the way that identity as show makers or as storytellers or dancers or performers filtered into a community [and] not just through the show. We really created something that never happened before.

Kerrie is an arts worker who was key to the successful development of NGAPARTJI NGAPARTJI.[1] Originally employed by Big hART as a choir coordinator for the Ernabella Women's Choir[2] on this project, Kerrie's ability to be 'with' these women and her natural affinity with the Pitjantjatjara language meant that she played a highly significant role in the project's development, coordination and successful delivery.

By way of context, NGAPARTJI NGAPARTJI was emblematic of what this form of participatory arts could be. Drawing from musical and storytelling workshops, and developing from deep relationships of trust with the community, it developed into a highly significant theatrical event that premiered at Melbourne International Arts Festival to consecutive sell-out crowds, then toured nationally to high critical acclaim.

Creating something new

NGAPARTJI NGAPARTJI was a remarkable achievement and I felt that participants were aware they were creating something new – recording songs, etc. at the time and when the show was touring I found that really profound. The Indigenous participants all say, 'We really did something new here. We really created something that had never happened before'. And that still rings true to me. There's this whole other story that Australia doesn't know. So while NGAPARTJI NGAPARTJI handed white audiences a catharsis on a plate – in some ways it was really simple, honest and brutal – but the complexity of the message was less understood.

But the show was only a part of the outcome, just the shiny bit that everybody remembers, where lots of people clap. The workshops and everything else were the bigger part. The most positive impacts were for the Indigenous participants, the women and young people who during the time of the project became much more confident in speaking their own minds to non-Indigenous people. They tended to socialise better too by the end with much less awkwardness and shyness when they got together. The most important identity building happened for the people of Ernabella in particular, for that community as well as for the individuals themselves. Their identity as show makers or as storytellers, dancers, performers all built in and filtered into the community, and not just through the show.

For me it was important to know the Indigenous language and it was essential to build truly collaborative ideas especially around song writing. In fact the musical outcomes wouldn't have happened if I hadn't spent the time just being with people and learning their language. Knowing the language meant I could give ideas permission and overcome participant shyness. So much of what happened flowed because I was able to spend time in community and with their language.

At the beginning, the workshops were providing profound experiences for non-Indigenous people working on the project but some of us, including me, became frustrated and cynical by the end of the project. There was the feeling that I was never being met halfway by participants especially around logistical details like dates, deadlines and so on.

There were tensions too around family demands which pulled people off task, and economic circumstances and welfare dependency was a problem. We had to watch white tutors especially if they were out of touch and came breezing into Indigenous communities thinking they know what the Aboriginals want. This approach doesn't ask participants to accept responsibility, and so they do too much for participants which finally did not enable them. My frustration built as the various parts of the project were seen by some participants and tutors as playtime – not essential, not a life necessity. I believed in and wanted an equal relationship with people but this did not come about as often as it should because there was not an equal investment from all participants.

I can see though that I did something unique with the music and films we recorded. And the collaborative song writing – there were no other young women writing songs. Songs weren't just raps over garage band beats, some of the songs they actually sang in the show were old people's. A core value has emerged I suppose – to let ideas breathe and to be able to feed back with improvements to build quality in the work.

Working on NGAPARTJI NGAPARTJI gave me the opportunity to have real life experiences with people from a different world view, expand my mind by learning about difference and language, sing in harmony and travel to beautiful places in the desert. But I'm not sure that the story is 100 per cent positive – and was never going to be. While NGAPARTJI NGAPARTJI can't change this problem, empowering people is good and the project could and did do that.

Where I've been for about a year is unable to talk about it. I've been deeply frustrated that I've been unable to articulate wisdom or learning or all of these things that people attach to me because of what I've done. It's something that I want and need to learn how to do, to learn how to articulate it all.

1   **Introduction**

In this chapter we turn our attention to the ART in Big hART. Of all the fields of practice and then sites where inquiry, story and expression are shared and change engendered, art is pre-eminent. Expressed differently, the centrality of art and art-making processes provide a consistent 'songline'³ through participatory arts projects as both points of connection and pathways through (Wright & Pascoe, 2015). This key notion is made visible by differing roles that are enacted in Big hART projects: participants, arts workers, cultural producers and artists themselves.

We do this in part by looking at Kerrie, who was an arts worker on one project. Through Kerrie's story we are able to see what it might mean when cultural learning and arts-based activities are used to develop the cultural literacies that are becoming increasingly important in times of globalisation (Jones, 2007), hyper-complexity and interconnectivity (Erstad, 2011; Qvortrup, 2003), and social dislocation (Miller, 2007). For example, creative activity is the medium through which culture both is created and can be understood. Kerrie's story also draws to our attention many of the tensions that exist when working in this participatory arts-based form in challenging contexts.

2   **The Arts as Signifiers and Enablers**

Following on from the introduction to the previous chapter, the arts, as expressive markers of culture, can become signifiers of diverse understandings, similarities and differences, and these can both help participants to belong, as well as to *resist* belonging. For example, learning language and knowing the history of the cultural block to which you belong in the case of NGAPARTJI

NGAPARTJI facilitates belonging, whereas in other projects such as DRIVE 'belonging' to a group where extreme risk taking was a badge of honour, or belonging to a group that was perceived by society as 'other' in a disparaging way because of low socio-economic status and dislocation, was resisted. This highlights that culture as expressed through the arts can not only be connecting, but also act as a disruption to the taken for granted or dimly understood.

3   Affordances and Constraints

When participants become art makers through a range of creative opportunities offered, there are three distinctive opportunities. First the arts can function as a tool to inspire and to educate, in this way being discursive, second, the arts function as a response to community challenges and impetus for community transformation and change that is didactic, and finally, the arts can function as pathways toward engagement and participation. The nexus of these actively draws together the different *forms* of social capital – bridging, bonding and linking – where 'bridging' links groups differentiated by difference (Putnam, 2000), 'bonding' occurs within groups (van Staveren & Knorringa, 2007), and 'linking' points to the power disparity that exists between individuals and groups with different levels of access and resources (Woolcock & Narayan, 2000). While these might not be mutually exclusive, but rather mutually reinforcing, what is key is the way each is relational and leads towards mutually beneficial outcomes (Cai, 2017).

4   Aesthetic Knowing

In participatory arts, the arts become pathways towards change through co-creation and creative inquiry (Kester, 2011). This potential for change lies in the ways in which aesthetic knowledge is experiential and affective. More specifically, this form of knowing and learning lies first in the way it is experiential or embodied, in other words the doing, and second, in knowing through feelings and experiences derived from the senses, that is, how these experiences may look, feel, smell, taste and sound.

Put differently, the arts become ways in which connections are made through producing, interpreting or presenting art to community that is aesthetic, cultural and political. Art is both the form that encodes meaning and the process through which meaning is made. At its best this is both socially relevant and constructively critical. This process is sometimes referred to as 'social aesthetics' or put differently 'a range of culturally patterned sensory experiences' (MacDougall, 2006, p. 2). In social aesthetics the sensory or aesthetic dimensions of a process or product permeate social relations through subjective experiences (Fahey, Prosser, & Shaw, 2015) where affect influences everyday life and decisions, reflecting the 'fragility of pure reason' and the power of affective knowledge (Corradi Fiumara, 2014).

Participatory arts is also grounded theoretically in 'relational aesthetics' (Bourriaud, 2002) with its emphasis on engagement and facilitating community among participants – makers and responders alike. Bourriaud defines this as 'a set of artistic practices which take as their departure the whole of human relations and their social context, rather than an independent and private space' (2002, p. 113). In this space that Bourriaud describes, what is important is what takes place between people, emphasising the social and event-bound forms of aesthetic experience (Holt, 2015).

The notion of multiple literacies[4] (New London Group, 1996) is also one helpful way of understanding the ecosystem of which Big hART is part and the somaesthetic affordances it provides. For example, this form of participatory arts practice, where professional artists and non-professional artists work together to create an artwork that neither could have realised alone (Matarasso, 2019), involves participants working as artists across different modalities and forms of expression, requiring differing forms of 'literacies' and embodied knowing. This form of arts practice is characterised by porous boundaries and by hybrid, cross-disciplinary and transdisciplinary practices, which exist in the liminal or the spaces in between. Put simply, participatory arts resists categorisation into neat conceptual labels or narrowly defined categories of practice and in this way can be thought of as transdisciplinary in nature, requiring broad sets of skills, knowledges and capabilities.

5   Productive Conditions, Practices and Possibilities

Informed by Kerrie's story and her experiences, we describe the productive conditions Big hART establishes, the practices it employs, and then the possibilities it engenders though these.

5.1   *Working as Artists*
Each of the socially critical and transformative possibilities that Big hART works towards occurs because participants act as artists, that is, they are makers of art through artistic processes. The acts of making require participants to use the senses, imagine, think and reason without having the 'answers' already

proscribed (Miller, Looney, & Siemens, 2011). This generative process develops a capacity for, and openness to, new experience through aesthetic means including an 'open space' for audiences to complete the experience, meaning that it is rich with productive possibilities. Simply put, in this context, participatory arts is a relational activity that seeks to (re)connect people through encounters and dialogues – the 'art of sociability'.

5.2   *Processes of Co-Creation*

Participatory arts feature the principles and processes of *co-creation* where the artwork – in whatever form is used to realise participants' experiences – is placed in the public domain, and *sense making* where it asks of us that we 'think, feel, talk and share in new ways with other people' (Matarasso, 2019, p. 50). Big *h*ART works in ways that make these principles manifest with a driving imperative to make art that is of a community and that has rich aesthetic qualities that stand up to scrutiny in high-profile venues such as international arts festivals and events. This means that the untold stories of community then have the capacity to engage and resonate with audiences beyond the site of origin. The outcome of this aesthetic and affective process for both participants and audiences is expansion of their expressive and perceptive possibilities, building capacity, knowledge and understanding and in these ways becoming a form of 'cultural activism' (Ozden Firat & Kuryel, 2011).

5.3   *Pluralistic Approaches to Development*

Kerrie's story contains rich layers of learning that go beyond the development of human capital, that is, an individual's capacity to compete in a global economy where work skills competencies preside (Wheelahan, 2017). Rather, Kerrie's story focuses on the development of human capabilities, reflecting a cosmopolitan approach that is more social and relational, less instrumental, and in this way more holistic, ethical and humanistic (Choo, 2018). This points to the way that participatory arts can lead to the engagement and development of human wellbeing with multiple and marginalised others in ethical ways, going beyond the entrepreneurial or workplace skills required to participate in the capitalist order and the associated reductive, more easily measurable competencies promoted by lists of twenty-first century skills (Soffel, 2016).

The latter approach misses the dispositions or values out of which people act. It focuses on the ends – in other words it targets symptoms such as lack of skills – rather than causes, that is, the values, attitudes and beliefs that promote the development of a labour force for the global economy. This reductive vision is promoted as *the* solution to the global forces reshaping the world, but it focuses on only one utilitarian element of globalisation (the economic) with no regard for social justice and participatory citizenship (Spring, 2015), missing the complexity of human living and what it might mean to thrive in in difficult and uncertain times (Fine, 2012; Macrine, 2009).

5.4   *Synergistic Pathways*

In order to understand this complex dynamic, and the roles people play, we need to foreground the way that participatory art brings together learning and creating, and the ways that these are both creative acts. Matarasso (2019) highlights, for example, that learning in, through and with art 'enables us, in different ways, to discover, process, understand, organise and share our experience' (p. 49), and this form of learning has potentiality, as when we create art 'we bring something into existence and in doing that we change the world' (p. 49). This highlights the power of art, for 'when we make sense of life, from feelings, ideas and experiences we may not even know we have, in forms to which others can respond creatively in turn, we conjure up new possibilities in all our imaginations' (p. 49). Kerrie sought to facilitate this potentiality for art to enable both actions and freedoms (Nussbaum, 2011) through her work as an arts worker on a project.

5.5   *Disruption and Disequilibrium*

Kerrie's story reveals the multidimensional nature of participatory arts projects, and the underlying tensions around them. Her uneasiness highlights not only what is gained through participatory arts, but also the costs, losses and unrealised opportunities often 'hidden' but present in creative and disruptive approaches (Ozden Firat & Kuryel, 2011).

When deeply considering Kerrie's story we are able to see how participatory arts draws on identity, and then links it with the performative (Alexander, Anderson, & Gallegos, 2005; Denzin, 2003). Performing, for example, literally provides visibility as does the process of exploring and 'trying on' a new role, in this way linking with becoming (Butler, 1990). Performing one's own story, often hidden or invisible, also allows others then to see something different. In NGAPARTJI NGAPARTJI, for example, Kerrie highlighted how 'a lot of different non-Indigenous people were able to have an insight into something that they otherwise wouldn't have in a way that they wouldn't otherwise have'. She elaborated: 'there is this whole other story that most of Australia doesn't know and I do think it's really profound, when that is able to get out there, you know, to the world'. Identity, as a fluid and motivational force, then can be constructed, shaped, formed and expressed through what one does and says, and in this way can be a force for social justice and awareness (Dimitriadis, 2009).

Kerrie also pointed to the power of creativity and the process of making something new through music and film workshops 'and time to let ideas breathe'.

Not only did this result in high-quality performance outcomes, but the process of developmental workshops engendered a process where 'we really did something new there. We really created something that never happened before'.

Across each of the three sites, the arts provided ways to connect to others through self-expression and relate through sharing ideas, experiences and meaningful interactions, but as Kerrie highlighted: 'But I'm not sure that the story is 100 per cent positive – and was never going to be. While NGAPARTJI NGAPARTJI can't change this problem, empowering people is good and the project could and did do that'.

This observation reminds us that, even with the best intentions, good will and determined effort, there will always be differences between expertise and privilege, and sites of contestation (Somerville, Davies, Power, Gannon, & de Carteret, 2011; Somerville & Perkins, 2003). This differential played out in unequal investments, making allowances, 'doing for', not holding people responsible, and 'never feeling like you're being met halfway by participants'. Put differently, there is a tension between providing support and letting participants both take and build responsibility.

5.6 *Strengthening an Expressive Life*

Finally, Ivey (2008) points to the importance of an 'expressive life', which describes access to the culture of the past, and our right to the creativity of both the present and the future. This highlights a broader understanding of culture – artistic, anthropological and political – and the ways in which it can reflect a constant conversation between people and ideas. At its best, an expressive life is full of affect and meaning, providing opportunities to connect to our various heritages and create new values in response. This means that we need spaces in which to renegotiate values, express beliefs, and to encounter those of others where equity, diversity and inclusion are key. Big *h*ART works towards this aspiration, going beyond simple instrumentalist understandings to what is a fundamental human and cultural right (United Nations, 1948, 2006) to lead productive and meaningful lives and to shape the culture of which we are part.

6 Conclusion

Through Kerrie's story we have foregrounded the role that the arts can play in participants' lives, recognising that this process is experiential, aesthetic and disruptive. Through the processes of engagement and participation and the intersection of trust and expertise, the quality of work was enhanced, stretching participants and arts workers in terms of their skills and knowledges, and strengthening their capabilities. However, such change can have not only benefits but also costs: at times the process becomes directive and sometimes workers do 'not feel ... that you are met halfway by participants'. In times where there is an increasing distrust of 'experts' it is also important to understand that there is power in expertise, both in disciplinary knowledge and trust, and this should not be discounted; the way that it is employed is critical.

Kerrie noted how the confluence of these participatory arts processes can result in a sense of achievement, pleasure and pride. In addition, through making hidden stories visible, Kerrie highlighted that high-performance outcomes can not only provide status and recognition, but also enable high levels of reciprocity and understanding when art is gifted back to the community in accessible ways.

The process was not always easy, never linear nor step-wise, and often challenging. Kerrie nonetheless noted:

> I can see that I actually did something unique ... and just certain ideas that were just dumb ideas at the time that turned into something because [they] came from conversations or shared humour or whatever it was that wouldn't have happened if I hadn't have had this extreme amount of energy to just hang out with people and learn a language and just spend time, you know, talking about stuff.

Kerrie's story highlights the in-between spaces of this project particularly, and participatory arts in general: 'it's not bread and butter and it's not band aids on open wounds. You know, it's ... it's ... it's playtime essentially, which is spiritual'.

Recognising and working with these multiple layers of complexity can lead to a 'wide-awakeness' and a more hopeful future where freedom is resistance, the arts generate possibilities, and work in progress is fuelled by the imagination (Greene, 1977, 1995; Pinar, 1998). Within these more relational and ethical frames, participatory arts, and Big *h*ART specifically, work with different ways of *thinking, being* and *becoming*. Following on from Corbett (2013), it is through openness and improvisation, empathy and flexibility, that we learn to face newness and difference in ideas, cultures, behaviours and technologies through joining in, learning new skills and experiences, and working as an artist through the processes of 'making' and 'performing' (Ennis & Tonkin, 2018).

Notes

1   NGAPARTJI NGAPARTJI was a multilayered project drawing on the APY Lands of central Australia comprising elements of raising the status and profile of Indigenous languages and

    providing young people with experience in the artistic world focusing on stage and perfor-
mance skills.

2 Ernabella is a remote Indigenous community in the central desert of Australia.

3 A concept drawn from Indigenous knowledges.

4 In this understanding literacies is taken to mean a plurality of approaches, texts and languages where there exists a knowledge, understanding and valuing of other cultures and a
capacity to express one's own culture functionally and critically. This means being active in
the ways that participants are able to generate, negotiate and enact their own understandings through being code breakers, text analysers, text meaning makers and text users across
multiple symbol systems (Freebody & Luke, 1990).

CHAPTER 6

Work, Security and Citizenship: Transitioning into the Workforce

> **Story:** BIG *h*ART provided a safe place – it is somewhere where everyone who is different can be – somewhere where being different is okay, but also knowing that everyone has something else to bring. (Kylie and Rachel, employment service workers)

Kylie and Rachel are employment service workers at Personnel Services, a nongovernment organisation (NGO) based in the regional town of Griffith in the Riverina Region of New South Wales. Griffith is a small regional city serving the local farming communities. Personnel Services is a not-for-profit organisation that tenders for placements from the Australian federal government and reports to the Department of Employment, Education and Workplace Relations. As an NGO, Personnel Services works in the local community to find jobs for young people and move them towards independent living. Kylie and Rachel's story reveals a great deal about the kinds of cultural processes involved in assisting young people like Jim and Billy into the adult world of work. Jim and Billy were involved in the GOLD project, which provided a creative and 'safe' space in which they could grow in confidence, find acceptance, develop social networks and negotiate paid employment. This is how Kylie and Rachel described the role of Big *h*ART in assisting Jim and Billy:

Providing safe spaces

> There was some cross-over between participants in GOLD and those who were clients of our service. One focus of the service is seeking to secure employment for those who are traditionally 'hard to place' because of their life circumstances. What we were able to see was the rebuilding of a positive youth identity through GOLD. It was Big *h*ART's processes that enabled Jim and Billy to connect with others, develop motivation and drive, and move towards successful independent living.
>
> One of the things that said to me the project had an impact was the fact that Jim put Chris as project Creative Producer down as a referee on his resume. This shows that it meant something to him. He obviously made a connection with the people involved in order to do that. Jim has

© KONINKLIJKE BRILL NV, LEIDEN, 2021 | DOI: 10.1163/9789004461574_006

Asperger's so he has never really fitted in. A lot of the time he has been on the end of bullying or a fight, mainly from being different. So that he has made a connection is quite significant, because so many people don't understand him or his personality. That is not an easy thing for him to do.

So now he is working at Target [a large retail shop], and there are still barriers. He can't read or write, so there was help needed to get him into that job, with his resume, the induction process, reading safety and hazard signs, etc. That is where we fitted in. And I don't think he would have had the motivation or drive to do that before Big hART. He has also completed the full six months with National Green Jobs Corp project and graduated from that. That happened after Big hART and I think that was what gave him the motivation and drive to give these things a go. He now lives out of home and is renting, so he is much more independent, he has his own place and his own job.

Billy got into his creativity through Big hART – he was a very withdrawn person, a bit of a loner. It was hard to engage even to get him to an appointment. He would always walk around with his music in his ears. He wasn't accepted for being different. There were a lot of anger issues with him. He has gone on to working lots of hours at Coles in the deli; we actually exited him from our service because he was well on his way to becoming independent. It helped with his confidence, and using his creativity, he grew into the person he wanted to be. Using his creativity really helped him with his anger issues; he was able to release them and engage his creativity, so a lot of these issues resolved because he got into the things he wanted to be. He certainly wouldn't have done this before [Big hART].

Billy's case, it was certainly a case of don't judge a book by its cover, he is a big burly bloke. He actually is in a customer service role now, and he is good at it. He has progressed and is living an independent life.

Big hART provided a safe place – it is somewhere where everyone who is different can be – somewhere where being different is okay, but also knowing that everyone has something else to bring. This demographic has had a lot of prior experiences of people being let down, it is part of their history, but Big hART really came through for them. What they did was provide access; there are not too many options here [in town]. You can go to the movies, but you need money to do that, and transport; there is only the pensioner or school bus.

Big hART offers something outside of the square; it is attractive to young people. It's listening to them, and asking them what they want to do. It's something that has meaning for them.

Kylie and Rachel's experience in the field affords an opportunity to see how community-based NGO workers understand the contribution of cultural practices to the life experience and opportunities available to marginalised young people like Jim and Billy. As front-line workers, they provide a unique perspective on the processes of identity formation in the context of broader shifts in the global economy. Kylie and Rachel's task is to assist young people to find employment in an increasingly precarious labour market. In this chapter, we drill down a little further to examine the kinds of productive conditions that need to be brought into existence to support young people as they navigate their way into the adult world. But first, we attempt to locate this kind of work in the context of broader shifts in the global economy and the impact it is having on young lives, especially in rural and regional communities.

1   **The Broader Context: Shifts in the Global Economy**

Today, young people like Jim and Billy face an increasingly fragile, uncertain and callous labour market. A cursory glance at recent media headlines in Australia, for example, tells us something about the precarious circumstances in which young people find themselves through no fault of their own:
- 'Insecure work the "new norm" as full-time job rate hits record low: report' (ABC News, 2018)
- 'Young and out: Australia's hidden scourge of youth unemployment' (Irvine, 2018)
- 'The PaTH [Prepare, Train, Hire] scheme is a farcical way to tackle youth unemployment' (Stewart, 2018)
- 'Long-term unemployment rates show the jobs picture is not rosy' (Jericho, 2018)
- 'The future of work will not be full-time' (Bessant, 2018)
- 'McDonald's accused of exploiting young workers with "learn and churn" practice' (Farrell & McDonald, 2018)
- 'Financial crisis hit young men hard – and they're yet to recover' (Wade, 2018)

Since the mid-1970s, the forces of globalisation, technology and neoliberalism have wreaked profound changes on society and the economy (Harvey, 2007). Nowhere is this more apparent than the youth labour market where the idea of permanent, secure and well-paid work is rapidly disappearing (Aronowitz & DiFazio, 2010). The evidence indicates that Australia now faces for the first time in its history a situation where most people in the workforce do not have full-time permanent jobs (Foundation for Young Australians, 2018). The shift towards market values and global production systems has led inexorably to flexible labour practices and the intensification of insecurity (Carney & Stanford, 2018). These shifts in the global labour market have been exacerbated by the emergence of developing economies in China, India, Russia and Eastern Europe, and recently Vietnam, Indonesia and Thailand. Together these economies have added 1.5 billion people to the labour force since 2000 (Standing, 2011, p. 28). Every country in the world now competes with all others for scarce capital investment and cheap labour supplies (Brown, Lauder, & Ashton, 2011).

The harsh reality is that only a minority of young people will succeed in the competition for the best jobs. For many young people, especially those living on the margins of society, the main avenue of employment is the service sector characterised by casualised, low-wage, contract and unskilled jobs (Furlong & Cartmel, 1997). Gorz (1997) puts it bluntly when he states that 'The society in which everyone could hope to have a place and a future marked out for him/her – the "work-based society", in which he/she could hope to have security and usefulness – is dead' (p. 57).

The upshot is that many young people are increasingly abandoned and held accountable for their own labour market fates (Furlong & Cartmel, 1997, p. 28). This reflects a broader set of market values (e.g., commodification, competition, privatisation and individualism) underpinned by a re-emergent neo-Darwinism ('survival of the fittest') in which only the most 'competent' will have jobs and the rest who do not have jobs are either incompetent or undeserving, or both (Bourdieu, 1998). Little wonder then that the language of 'wasted lives' (Bauman, 2004), 'collateral damage' (Bauman, 2011), 'disposability' and 'culture of cruelty' (Giroux, 2012) are summoned to describe the ways in which young people are being treated and left behind.

The impact of these global labour force dynamics on individual lives is exacerbated by one's social class, gender, race and geographic location. All projects involved in this research have occurred in communities where the ravages of neoliberalism have been most acutely felt in terms of diminishing job opportunities and a range of indicators of social disadvantage, such as high levels of unemployment, poor educational participation and retention rates, low school completion and achievement levels, social welfare dependency, high rates of crime and delinquency, poor mental health and illness, youth suicide, and drug and alcohol abuse (Vinson, 2007).

Under these circumstances young people can easily be stigmatised as the 'problem'. Deficit views and victim-blaming discourses abound as Gen Y are labelled in derogatory and demeaning terms (e.g., 'unproductive', 'lazy', 'unmotivated', 'at risk', 'troublemakers', 'irresponsible' and 'dumb') (Valencia, 2010). As Grossberg (2005) argues:

> It has become common to think of kids as a threat to the existing social order and for kids to be blamed for the problems they experience. We slide from kids in trouble, kids have problems, and kids are threatened, to kids as trouble, kids as problems, and kids as threatening. (p. 16)

In response, it is hardly surprising to find rising levels of anger, anxiety, aliena-tion and anomie as young people experience a heightened sense of despair and hopelessness about their economic futures (Standing, 2011). Against this backdrop, the research on which this book is based seeks to generate some alternative possibilities based on the experiences of young people themselves as they attempt to re-imagine their futures through participatory arts. The pur-pose is to move beyond the limitations of deficit discourses by locating indi-vidual troubles (e.g., unemployment) in relation to broader economic, political and social forces at play, and not simply focus on the personal situation and character of individuals (e.g., blaming the victim) (Mills, 1971).

A central argument throughout this book is that young people require creative spaces in which they can develop the capabilities to help them: (i) identify the kind of lives they want to lead; (ii) acquire the skills and knowledge to achieve their goals; and (iii) realise the political, social and economic circumstances which enable them (Sen, 1992; see also Down, Smyth, & Robinson, 2018). We shall expand on this capabilities approach in Chapter 7.

As we delve into the lives of young participants like Jim and Billy we find evidence of a number of cultural processes which allow them to:

- re-write/right their identities in more empowering ways;
- make things of interest to sell, thus building an entrepreneurial spirit and sense of accomplishment;
- enrol in further education and training to enhance their credentials and skills;
- develop employability skills such as public speaking, confidence, teamwork, creativity, and organisational and planning skills;
- enhance their writing and literacy skills;
- cultivate social networks and support structures; and
- develop a greater sense of agency.

In the remainder of this chapter we explain these outcomes by looking at the kinds of productive practices that enable young people to flourish in adverse circumstances.

2   Productive Practices

Drawing on Kylie and Rachel's story, in this chapter we identify and describe a number of cultural and pedagogical practices that enable organisations like Big *h*ART to make a difference in the lives of marginalised young people.

2.1   Challenging 'Deficit' Thinking

Kylie and Rachel were able to cut through deficit ways of thinking when they stated that 'Big hART provided a safe place – it is somewhere where everyone who is different can be – somewhere where being different is okay, but also knowing that everyone has something else to bring'. This is an unambiguous statement about the pivotal importance of challenging deficit views about young people. As Maxine Greene (2001a) argues, labels 'carry the messages of power: they demean, they exclude; they create stereotypes' (p. xvi). The problem is that they 'become a part of our lived experience; they can become a part of one's life, one's identity and hence, difficult to replace' (Hudak, 2001, p. 9). If we are going to advance the employment prospects of marginalised young people, then there are clear benefits to be gained by starting with a more optimistic and humane view about their potential.

As noted earlier, deficit views are based on the assumption that young people fail to find jobs because of internal deficits rather than locating the problem within the context of broader shifts in the global labour market and institutional life. The influential American sociologist C. Wright Mills (1959/1971) explains this line of reasoning better than most when he argues that 'personal troubles' are best understood in the context of 'public issues', by which he means 'the larger structure of social and historical life' (p. 15). In the case of unemployment, he explains it this way:

> The very structure of opportunities has collapsed. Both the correct statement of the problem and the range of possible solutions require us to consider the economic and political institutions of the society, and not merely the personal situation and character of a scatter of individuals. (1959/1971, p. 15)

According to Kylie and Rachel, Big hART challenges this kind of deficit thinking by seeing young people 'at promise' rather than as bundles of pathologies to be 'fixed'. It draws on young people's knowledge, experience, language and interests to create enriched programs, activities and opportunities (Swadener, 1995) with a view to effecting personal and social change (Shor, 1992; Oakes, Rogers, & Lipton, 2006). As Kylie and Rachel noted, this kind of approach is 'outside of the square, Big hART came through for them, it gave them confidence'.

2.2   Moving beyond the Self-Fulfilling Prophecy

Young people like Jim and Billy are typically streamed (or tracked) into low-level competency-based vocational courses on the basis that they lack intelligence, ability and/or motivation (Oakes, 2005). Once streamed, future pathways and possibilities are foreclosed as they assume limiting identities (e.g., 'practical', 'non-academic' or 'troublemaker'). Mike Rose's (1989) brilliant book *Lives on the boundary* portrays the damage wrought on young people by these impoverished views of human potential and the dehumanising educational practices that flow from them. Rose (1989) believes that, despite the best efforts of many fine programs and teachers, vocational education 'is most often a place for those who are just not making it, a dumping ground for the disaffected' (p. 26). He goes on to explain how this works for those kids deemed to be inferior and less capable than the smarter kids:

> If you're a working-class kid in the vocational track, the options you'll have to deal with this will be constrained in certain ways: You're defined by your school as 'slow'; you're placed in a curriculum that isn't designed to liberate you but to occupy you, or if you're lucky, train you, though the training is for work the society does not esteem; other students are picking up the cues from your school and your curriculum and interacting with you in particular ways. (1989, p. 28)

Rose (1989) recounts the story of Ken Harvey, a young vocational education student who said: 'I just want to be average'. Rose describes his own dismay on hearing such comments. 'That woke me up', he said (p. 28). He elaborates:

> What Ken and so many others [like Jim and Billy] do is protect themselves from such suffocating madness by taking on with a vengeance the identity implied in the vocational track. Reject the confusion and frustration by openly defining yourself as the Common Joe. Champion the average. Rely on your own good sense. Fuck this bullshit. Bullshit, of course, is everything you – and the others – fear is beyond you: books, essays, tests, academic scrambling, complexity, scientific reasoning, philosophical inquiry. (1989, p. 29)

In countering these kinds of deleterious experiences, Rose (1989) describes the profound influence of his college teacher Jack McFarland who 'caught my fancy and revitalized my mind – what I felt now was something further, some recognition that an engagement with ideas could foster competence and lead me out into the world' (p. 47). Like Jack McFarland, Big *h*ART workers including producers, directors, artists, performers and technicians offer an alternative set of possibilities by acknowledging that all young people are in the process of 'becoming somebody' (Wexler, 1992). They use their artistic and technical talents in collaboration with local communities to create cultural settings and performances that assist young people to build confidence, experience, relationships, capabilities and knowledge in more empowering ways. In the tradition of Paulo Freire (1970/2000),

> people develop their power to perceive critically the way they exist in the world with which and in which they find themselves; they come to see the world not as a static reality, but as a reality in process, in transformation. (p. 83)

Therefore, it was not surprising to hear Kylie and Rachel talk optimistically about the impact of the GOLD project in building strengths and capabilities and assisting young people to re-imagine their futures in new ways. We heard comments from participants like: 'Really, it has led to my job ... where I am now'; 'I just thought, wow, I would like to own my own clothing company'; and 'She actually does a full-time course at TAFE now to do her Aged Care [Certificate]'. These young people are learning to not only survive but thrive by asserting power and control over their lives. Their stories allow us to interrupt the demeaning and damaging view that some young people are unfit or incapable of using their intellect and creative energies (Sennett, 2006).

As Greene (1995) argues so eloquently, the use of artistic imagination can foster a 'full range of human intelligence' by developing multiple languages including 'imagery', 'body movement' and 'musical sound' which provide young people with opportunities 'to name their worlds' (p. 57) and 'perhaps, transform to some degree their lived world' (p. 48).

2.3 Understanding the Complexity of Young Lives

At the heart of Kylie and Rachel's story is the acknowledgment of the complexity of young lives. Jim was dealing with issues related to Asperger's syndrome; thus he 'never really fitted in'. As a consequence, he was subjected to bullying and isolation at school. Big hART provided a safe space in which he could flourish and, in the words of Kylie and Rachel, the fact 'that he has made a connection is quite significant, because so many people don't understand him or his personality'. As Smyth (2016) argues, how young people respond to school depends on their personal, family and health-related histories, which can be complex and messy and may not always 'fit well with middle-class sensibilities' (p. 221).

Consistent with effective participatory arts practice, Big hART acknowledges and welcomes young people no matter what their circumstances and is prepared to work with multiple and complex forms of disadvantage including health, poverty, housing, ethnicity, trauma, transience and so on. Furthermore, it acknowledges that young people often present with incomplete and less than satisfying experiences of schooling as well as the need for care and safety. In these circumstances, the priority is providing innovative practices that re-engage them in socially worthwhile activities over which they have control and ownership and see relevance (Smyth & McInerney, 2012).

In this context, Greene (1995) argues that we need to keep 'visions of possibility before our eyes in the face of rampant carelessness and alienation and fragmentation' (p. 197). She expands further on this critically informed and humane way of working with young people:

> And, yes, it is to work for responsiveness to principles of equity, principles of equality, and principles of freedom, which still can be named within contexts of caring and concern. The principles and the contexts have to be chosen by living human beings against their own life-worlds and in light of their lives with others, by persons able to call, to say, to sing, and – using their imaginations, tapping their courage – to transform. (1995, p. 198)

In pursuing this more hopeful vision, Greene (1995) outlines a set of democratic principles to guide the ways in which organisations work with young people. Drawing on Hannah Arendt (1961), she argues that what the world requires now is 'the possibility of shared commitments' based on a willingness to come together through dialogue and the 'continuing constitution and renewal of a common world' (1995, p. 196). She believes that this kind of shared responsibility provides opportunities to build 'networks of concern in which we ... create and recreate ourselves' (p. 197).

In pursuing this agenda, Big hART, like Stanton-Salazar (1997), adopts a 'network-analytic approach' to provide opportunities for young people to enter into 'different social and institutional contexts' in which they can form relationships with 'agents who exert various degrees of control over institutional resources' (e.g., bureaucratic influence, career information, training and mentorship) (p. 4). Based on the evidence of Kylie and Rachel, organisations like Big hART play a pivotal role in this kind of capacity building and networking for marginalised young people by 'helping them to connect with others'.

With the rise of a new 'precariat class' of disaffected youth who have no secure identity or sense of purpose in life other than survival and short-termism (Standing, 2011) there is a growing urgency to reconnect marginalised young people to learning via arts-based community-based activities such as LUCKY, GOLD and NGAPARTJI NGAPARTJI (see Chapter 1). In the Australian context, Big hART plays a pivotal role in producing high-quality artistic performances which connect, engage and inspire young people. This is achieved by providing access and connection to expert mentors who are able to, in the words of Kylie and Rachel, 'develop motivation and drive, and move [participants] towards successful independent living'.

2.4   Providing Opportunities for 'Good' Work

Whilst Kylie and Rachel are keen to help Jim and Billy transition into paid employment (or any kind of job for that matter) with the best intentions, there is a danger that far too many young people are shunted into low-level, poorly paid and demeaning jobs. Predictably, young people like Jim and Billy are often pushed out of school and confined to the ranks of the unemployed and/or consigned to poorly paid 'contingent', 'disposable' and 'temporary' jobs (McLaren & Farahmandpur, 2005, p. 44). In the words of Kylie and Rachel,

> This demographic has had a lot of prior experiences of people being let down, it is part of their history, but Big *h*ART really came through for them. What they did was provide access; there are not too many options here [in town].

In light of the limited job opportunities available in Griffith, it is hardly surprising that Jim and Billy were placed in retail service jobs at Target and Coles supermarkets respectively. Whilst Kylie and Rachel have achieved positive outcomes in terms of their remit to move unemployed young people into jobs and independent living, there still lingers the larger question of what kind of work is desirable and for whom? In short, there is a need to consider how young people are engaged, or not, in meaningful and rewarding work rather than just getting a job in order to survive, as important as this may be in these uncertain times.

Drawing on Kincheloe's aptly titled books *Toil and trouble: Good work, smart workers, and the integration of academic and vocational education* (1995) and *How do we tell the workers: The socioeconomic foundations of work and vocational education* (1999), there is an important distinction to be made between 'work' and a 'job'. According to Kincheloe (1999), 'A job is simply a way of making a living; work involves a sense of completion and fulfilment' (p. 64). Pursuing this line of argument, 'good' work is socially worthwhile, ethically grounded, democratic and fulfilling in the way it contributes to human betterment and growth. It involves a strong belief in 'worker dignity' (p. 65) whereby all work should involve elements of learning, self-direction, joy, variety, cooperation, self-fulfilment and democracy (see Down et al., 2018, pp. 55–56 for discussion). This more expansive and socially just understanding of 'good work' creates the foundations on which to build a set of new possibilities based on what Bauman (2004) calls a 'life project' involving 'self-esteem', 'self-determination' and 'long-term security' (p. 151).

Central to all three Big hART projects involved in this research is a desire to assist young people to develop the kinds of capabilities and understandings that will enable them to realise their dreams, desires and aspirations for their imagined futures. This involves a better understanding of the circumstances in which they find themselves in order to bring about personal and social change. In the process, participants acquire a range of creative technical and performance skills related to digital media, art, radio, theatre, communication and filmmaking. These new-found skills are fostered in the context of addressing real community problems (e.g., struggling teenage mothers, elderly people living in isolation, and drug addiction and suicide – LUCKY; isolation and alienation among struggling farming families – GOLD; and preservation of cultural knowledge and language – NGAPARTJI NGAPARTJI: see Chapter 1), which helps to create a spirit of civic engagement, belongingness and connectedness among participants.

In other words, young people are actively engaged in 'good work' characterised by a sense of relevance, imagination, ethics, cooperation, democracy and human betterment. Sadly, for many young people today, these kinds of principles and values are seldom realised in the 'new work order' (Gee, Hull, & Lankshear, 1996), which is increasingly characterised by insecurity, repetitiveness, boredom, low-level skills, poor pay and casualisation (Sennett, 2006). Put simply, the private market is either unable or unwilling to provide enough jobs, let alone good jobs, especially in those communities ravaged by the forces of globalisation and deindustrialisation (Agger, 2004).

2.5   Developing Engaged Citizenship

In this context, Big hART, like many organisations working with marginalised youth, faces the contradictory role of assisting young people technically for the world of work (i.e., 'getting a job') and, at the same time, providing them with the knowledge and skills to become critically engaged citizens. Freire (1998) explains this problem well when he describes the importance of an education which includes not only 'technical and scientific preparation' but 'speaks of the workers' presence in the world' (p. 92). For Freire, education is more than simply 'training' young people like Jim and Billy for whatever jobs are available. It involves an ethical responsibility to equip young people with the knowledge, skills and dispositions 'to contest workplace inequalities, imagine democratically organized forms of work, and identify and challenge those injustices that contradict and undercut the most fundamental principles of freedom, equality, and respect for all people who constitute the global public sphere' (Giroux, 2012, p. 9).

We can now begin to see how Big *h*ART projects open up some radically different ways of conceptualising citizenship by creatively engaging young people in community-owned projects of immediate relevance and social worth. Through these experiences they are learning about the spirit of NGA-PARTJI NGAPARTJI, meaning 'I give you something. You give me something'. This way of being takes us beyond the limitations of market values and human capital formation to establish bonds that link people together materially, socially and emotionally. This approach, according to Greene (1995), requires a new social imagination, one founded on: (i) a spirit of interconnectedness and communion (p. 33); (ii) decency, humaneness, awareness and meaning (p. 35); (iii) solidarity and dialogue (p. 39); and (iv) plurality and difference (p. 42).

We can see elements of these values in Kylie and Rachel's story, which suggests a shared commitment, concern and care toward both Jim and Billy who did not seem to 'fit in'. We hear how Jim 'made a connection with the people [at Big *h*ART]' and Billy 'grew into the person he wanted to be'. Kylie and Rachel explained how 'Big hART offers something outside of the square; it is attractive to young people. It's listening to them, and asking them what they want to do. It's something that has meaning for them'. Herein lies the essence of a more engaged citizenship that speaks powerfully to a different kind of world in which young people are treated with mutual respect, trust and care.

3   Conclusion

In this chapter, we have argued that wider shifts in the global economy are having profound effects on young people's lives, especially those living in circumstances of poverty and disadvantage. We examined the implications for two young people – Jim and Billy – by listening to the story of two employment service workers – Kylie and Rachel –who worked for an NGO in the small regional town of Griffith, New South Wales. Their story provided an opportunity to examine some of the challenges involved in assisting young people like Jim and Billy into paid employment and the role of Big *h*ART in creating the kinds of cultural and pedagogical practices conducive to supporting the process of re-engagement and transformation.

We extrapolated a number of things from Kyle and Rachel's experience. Firstly, young people need to be known well, respected and trusted. Secondly, they require 'safe' spaces where they are welcome and belong for who they are. Thirdly, judgements should be suspended as all young people are seen as 'at promise' rather than as bundles of pathologies. Fourthly, young people need spaces where they can engage in socially worthwhile activities that have personal meaning. And finally, should have the opportunity to re-write their identities in ways that allow them to pursue their dreams, desires and aspirations for their imagined future.

Specifically, Kylie and Rachel identified a range of social, economic and personal benefits for participants involved with Big hART's GOLD project. These ranged from the acquisition of employability skills related to reading and writing, self-confidence and public speaking, to technical skills such as jewellery making, photography and lighting, to developing social networks and support structures, and confidence to undertake TAFE courses related to specific careers. One of the participants summed up her renewed sense of optimism and hope in the following words:

> When I started going to Big hART I didn't really have any future goals … I suppose because I was young and, you know, didn't really see into the future … You know, but then I just thought, wow, I would like to own my own clothing company … have my own clothing line. It was good.

CHAPTER 7

Capabilities and Informal Learning Spaces: Creating a 'Life Project'

Story: I slow myself down a bit and listen to others. (Mick)

Mick was directed to Big *h*ART by the police after becoming involved in criminal activity. He described the positive impact that Big *h*ART had on his life. His involvement in the DRIVE project allowed him both to strengthen his creativity and to develop a set of capabilities including technical skills that he otherwise would not have. Importantly, he was able to think about himself and others in different ways. The ability to think reflectively about life's experiences and events was a powerful learning opportunity for Mick. His story reminds us about the importance of 'hanging in' with young people doing it tough, no matter what their background or circumstances. It also reveals a great deal about the relational dimensions of learning whereby people desire a sense of connectedness and belongingness around common interests and concerns in order to make a difference. This is how Mick described his experience:

Sure I can do that

I became involved with Big *h*ART after a cop caught me getting into mischief. I was bored and breaking into classrooms at the local school in an attempt to steal and hock their computers. I had a bit of a drug problem. I didn't know what I was doing, or where I was going. I was lost. When she caught me she thought I had nothing else to do and I needed something to keep me out of trouble. They basically told me they were going to take me somewhere, to see if I could learn something from these people. 'Which people?' Big *h*ART. They told me all about it and I said I'd give it a go.

When I went to Big *h*ART, they asked if I could paint caravans. I said, 'Sure, I can do that'. Then they asked if I could put lights on caravans. I said, 'Yeah, I can. No worries'. It was my first involvement in a Big *h*ART show. I've been involved now for six years at a technical level, with sets, lighting and sound. Before Big *h*ART I couldn't work a video camera, I couldn't even hop on a computer hardly. But they got professionals to come and show me how to do things. When they showed me I just knew how to do it. I've tried to cherish everything they taught me.

Another thing that's made a big impact on me is listening to the stories of people in the shows we put on. The DRIVE project had the biggest impact. I was doing sound for that, and when I was doing that I listened to the stories, and these affected me, especially the Hicks story. He had everything, just got himself and had almost finished apprenticeship, and was working real hard. He fell asleep while behind the steering wheel and hit the back of a truck. It was kind of disturbing hearing about how he was still alive and how he was crushed between the two cars. He lifted his head up and said he was sorry to the truck driver. And when I heard that, it was devastating to me. Just imagine the truck driver. It wasn't his fault. He was just driving round the corner.

I learnt about others too. You've got to really put yourself aside a bit, when you work with other people. I slow myself down a bit and listen to others. It's more about listening to other people.

1   Introduction

We draw on Mick's story to illustrate how the arts and informal learning spaces can support young people to develop the capabilities, knowledge and skills to address the obstacles and barriers they face in life. The purpose of this chapter is twofold, firstly, to describe the kinds of learning that actually take place, largely from the point of view of participants like Mick, and secondly, to identify the particular cultural, relational, organisational and pedagogical conditions that enable it to happen. It is important to note that Big hART typically works with young people who are disengaged and alienated from formal educational institutions. Unfortunately, there are escalating numbers of young people who no longer look to school as a venue in which the creative spirit can be nurtured, as evidenced by a general malaise – low-quality work, absenteeism, drug and alcohol abuse, loss of meaning and purpose in education, and cognitive illness (Kincheloe, 1995; Brock & Goodman, 2013). There is mounting evidence that a 'standardised curriculum gives nonstandard students no place to go' (Ohanian, 1999, p. 2).

Speaking about young people like Mick, Herbert Kohl (1994) urges us not to see failure as some kind of personal deficit or pathology but instead, 'the frustrated will to know' (p. 6). In his words, 'failure results from a mismatch between what the learner wants to do and is able to do' (p. 6). In response, Big hART seeks to create alternative spaces and places where young people have an opportunity to re-engage in learning and community life through arts-based projects. In these informal spaces, young people are provided with the emotional, intellectual and creative resources to develop capabilities to enhance their definition of self, inner satisfaction and agency (Akom, 2007).

Consistent with participatory arts and underpinning Big hART's approach is the view that all young people, given the appropriate cultural and pedagogical settings, are willing to learn and capable of learning. This approach challenges some deeply entrenched views about failure and the willingness of young people to engage in learning. It also challenges the view that those young people who are 'dropping out', 'drifting off', and/or 'being excluded' are somehow deficient in terms of language, experience, strengths, knowledge and resources (Smyth & Hattam, 2014).

Perhaps the best way to describe Big hART's approach to learning is to draw on Amartya Sen's (1992) notion of capabilities, which offers a much richer perspective on how arts-based practices can assist young people to identify the kinds of lives they want to lead; provide them with the skills and knowledge to go about it; and help them understand the cultural, economic and political circumstances that either enable or impede them (Smyth et al., 2010, p. 74).

In essence, Big hART takes a transformative approach to help young people move beyond limiting deficit and scripted ways of being in the world (e.g. 'at risk', 'lazy', 'low achiever', 'disadvantaged', 'troublesome', 'non-academic', 'single mum', 'unemployed' and so on) and instead, to take on more powerful identities as smart workers and creative critically engaged citizens. Big hART achieves this by building humanising relationships and mobilising collective action around relevant, meaningful and worthwhile community projects. In this environment young people feel safe to take risks, ownership and social action.

As we excavate the narratives of the young people involved in this research we find evidence of a wide range of learning, from the acquisition of fundamental life skills including improved social skills, decision making, problem solving and information technology (e.g. audio visual, camera, sound, editing and so on) to imagining new identities and futures. By way of summary, there is evidence of positive impacts in terms of:
- exploring future educational options
- developing confidence to speak publicly
- developing organisational and planning skills
- problem solving and teamwork
- writing and literacy skills
- developing social skills
- pursuing passions and interests
- developing a sense of self-efficacy.

Whilst basic life skills related to reading, writing and numeracy cannot be taken for granted, the participants in these projects were learning a great deal more as they re-wrote their identities in new and creative ways. For many participants, their involvement in Big hART provided a rare opportunity to challenge some damaging and deficit images of themselves as they began the journey of re-invention based on a sense of hope, optimism and agency. We gain a sense of how this transformational learning occurs in small but profoundly influential ways through the narrative of Mick, a young man searching for a fresh start.

2 Productive Practices

At heart, Mick's story reveals how learning is a social practice in which individuals come together to understand themselves and their world with a view to improving the way things are. Big *h*ART develops opportunities for young people like Mick to reconnect with learning in ways that honour the civic and democratic purposes of education envisaged by educators such as John Dewey (1916/1944). Drawing on Mick's narrative, it is possible to identify and describe some of the productive practices that enable Big *h*ART to connect to the lives of young people in ways that enable more emancipatory forms of learning to occur.

2.1 *Developing a Capabilities Approach*

What we have heard from Mick and other young people throughout this book is the importance of developing what Walker (2006) refers to as 'multi-dimensional capabilities', which encompass: social relations and networks; the capability to be a friend and mentor; respect and recognition; self-confidence and self-esteem; aspiration and motivation; health and wellbeing; emotional safety; and voice. Once these capabilities are in place, young people are far more likely to re-engage in learning and the task of building a 'life project' involving 'self-esteem', 'self-determination' and 'long-term security' (Bauman, 2004, p. 151).

Sen (1992) provides some important insights into the idea of capabilities, which he describes as those 'valuable functionings that make up our lives, and more generally, our freedom to promote objectives we have reasons to value' (p. 3). Pivotal to this broader project is 'the quality (the "well-ness", as it were) of the person's being' (p. 39). According to Sen, this sense of wellbeing involves 'a set of interrelated functionings, consisting of beings and doings' (p. 39). These 'functionings', Sen (1992) argues, range from the most basic needs, such as being well-nourished and avoiding premature morbidity and/or mortality, to more sophisticated achievements like self-respect and being able to take part in the life of the community (p. 5).

Walker (2006) expands this description by identifying eight dimensions of the capabilities approach to social justice pedagogy. It is worth quoting these eight dimensions at length:

1. *Autonomy*, being able to have choices, having information on which to make choices, planning a life after school, reflection, independence, empowerment.

2. *Knowledge*, of school subjects which are intrinsically interesting or instrumentally useful for post-school choices of study, paid work and a career, girls' access to all school subjects, access to powerful analytical knowledge, and including knowledge of girls' and women's lives, knowledge for critical thinking and for debating complex moral and social issues, knowledge from involvement in intrinsically interesting school societies, active inquiry, transformation of understanding, fair assessment/examination of knowledge gained.

3. *Social relations*, the capability to be a friend, the capability to participate in a group for friendship and for learning, to be able to work with others to solve problems and tasks, being able to work with others to form effective or good groups for learning and organizing life at school, being able to respond to human need, social belonging.

4. *Respect and recognition*, self-confidence and self-esteem, respect for and from others, being treated with dignity, not being diminished or devalued because of one's gender, social class, religion or race, valuing other languages, other religions and spiritual practice and human diversity, showing imaginative empathy, compassion, fairness and generosity, listing to and considering other persons' points of view in dialogue and debate in and out of class in school, being able to act inclusively.

5. *Aspiration*, motivation to learn and succeed, to have a better life, to hope.

6. *Voice*, for participation in learning, for speaking out, not being silenced through pedagogy or power relations or harassment, or excluded from curriculum, being active in the acquisition of knowledge.

7. *Bodily integrity and bodily health*, not to be subjected to any form of harassment at school by peers or teachers, generally being safe at school, making own choices about sexual relationships, being able to be free from sexually transmitted diseases, being involved in sporting activities.

8. *Emotional integrity and emotions*, not being subject to fear which diminishes learning, either from physical punishment or verbal attacks, developing emotions and imagination for understanding, empathy, awareness and discernment. (pp. 179–180)

Returning to Mick's narrative for a moment, he reminds us that all learners are individuals with unique sets of needs, desires and aspirations. We cannot take anything for granted in terms of what young people bring to the table. Their lives are often complex, messy and unpredictable and these circumstances require a different kind of learning, one grounded in relational trust, respect, mutuality, social relationships, voice, flexibility and meaningful tasks.

2.2 Building Relationships That Are Inclusive, Engaging and Enabling

If learning is to occur, then appropriate cultural processes are required that are inclusive of all (irrespective of circumstances), engaging and enabling. Creating spaces of this kind is no easy task. More specifically, it requires a consistent set of guiding principles, values and protocols founded on a deep belief in the value of individuals and their capabilities to succeed in careers, family and life. Furthermore, this inclusive and creative approach needs to be linked to a philosophy of learning that challenges the way things are, and as such is able to generate alternative realities and possibilities for the individual and community. For example, the DRIVE project focused on the issue of male adolescence in remote areas and the high rate of autocide (young men self-harming in motor vehicle smashes) on Tasmanian roads. Mick, along with 96 other young men, engaged in workshops where they learnt a range of skills in sound recording, filmmaking, interviewing, storytelling and digital production. These workshops involved artists, filmmakers, skaters, beat boxers, sound artists, designers, illustrators, dancers and musicians, who all added their expertise to the final film production.

Mick recollected a significant moment in his own self-reflection around an incident in the DRIVE project involving the tragic death of a young person in his local community. Mick explained:

> He lifted his head up and said he was sorry to the truck driver. And when I heard that, it was devastating to me. Just imagine the truck driver. It wasn't his fault. He was just driving round the corner.

This kind of transformational learning is based on a different kind of politics and social imaginary guided by the values of inclusivity, engagement and social action to address local questions, concerns and problems.

2.3 Creating Dialogic Spaces for Identity Work

Young people require spaces where they feel safe to explore identities. As Mick explained, 'I didn't know what I was doing, or where I was going. I was lost'. These spaces privilege the voices of young people, what engages them, what is real, and what is relevant to their lives. In other words, they start from where young people are at in terms of their culture, language, experience and interests. This requires the creation of dialogic spaces where young people can come together as equals in search of meaning about their world and the things that matter to them. Mick's experience points to the absolute importance of valuing people's knowledge and experience. In his words: 'When I went to Big *h*ART, they asked if I could paint caravans. I said, "Sure, I can do that". Then they asked if I could put lights on caravans. I said, "Yeah, I can. No worries"'. It is this horizontal relationship based on mutual respect between participants and what they bring to the learning encounter that really matters.

What we are alluding to here is what Akom (2007) describes as 'free spaces' which share some of the following characteristics:

> A sense of shared bonds, places to revive one's culture, places to rejuvenate our spirits, participatory and democratic spaces, places to civically engage-debate-dialogue, places to form social networks, places to educationally achieve, places to form democratic or revolutionary visions of social change, places to recover and enjoy group identity, places to cultivate self and communal respect, cooperation, and community uplift. (pp. 612–613)

For Akom (2007), 'Free spaces represents an intellectual and political project created to reveal and theorize the social and cultural production of "ordinary people" who have been relegated to the margins' (p. 611). We take from Akom the understanding that 'all spaces are politicized, racialized, and gendered, insofar as they are infused with questions of power and privilege' (p. 611). Significantly though, these spaces become the 'launching points for transformative resistance and social change' (p. 613).

2.4 *Interrupting Dominant Constructions of Self and Youth Identity*
If learning is to be truly transformational it requires opportunities for young people to interrupt dominant images of self and youth identity. Given the power of mass media and advertising to shape young lives in largely negative ways, including racism, sexism, homophobia, materialism and violence, it should be hardly surprising that young people's personal identity and sense of self-worth are often damaged. Drawing on Maxine Greene (1995), we believe that projects like DRIVE provide the 'public spaces in which students speaking in their own voices and acting on their own initiatives, can identify themselves and choose themselves in relation to such principles as freedom, equality, justice and concern for others' (p. 68). When Mick first joined Big *h*ART he was acutely aware of his own limitations: 'Before Big *h*ART I couldn't work a video camera, I couldn't even hop on a computer hardly'. Transformational learning

of the kind advocated by Big *h*ART endeavours to help young people like Mick to re-write their identities as part of an ongoing process of personal and social transformation by working from weakness to strength and, in the process, 'becoming somebody, to establish their identity through social relations' (Wexler, 1992, p. 156).

2.5   *Remaking Individual Lives in Communities of Practice*

Mick's narrative reminds us of the importance of connecting young people to communities of practice. In Mick's case, Big *h*ART was the last port of call. There was nowhere else for him to go. In his words, 'I was bored and breaking into classrooms at the local school in an attempt to steal and hock their computers. I had a bit of a drug problem'. Big *h*ART offered Mick a place where he could reconnect to community, where he could develop relationships, feel welcome and belong. What is apparent in Mick's story is the value of linking the process of individual learning to communities of practice based on shared values and a commitment to each other.

Wenger's (1998) seminal writing on the notion of communities of practice is instructive in relation to Mick's involvement with the DRIVE project. Wenger (1998) identifies three aspects of communities of practice: firstly, 'mutual engagement' of participants whereby meanings are negotiated with one another (p. 73); secondly, the 'negotiation of a joint enterprise', which takes account of the 'full complexity of mutual engagement' (p. 77) as well as 'the resources and constraints of their situations' (p. 79); and thirdly, the development of 'a shared repertoire', which includes 'routines, words, tools, ways of doing things, stories, gestures, symbols, genres, actions or concepts the community has produced' (p. 83). Mick acknowledged the influence of connecting to this community of practice through mentors and experts in his own journey: 'But they got professionals to come and show me how to do things. When they showed me I just knew how to do it. I've tried to cherish everything they taught me'. At the heart of this pedagogical work is a desire to transform inequitable and oppressive institutions and social relations so that individuals can learn, grow and develop to their full potential together as a community of practice.

2.6   *Researching Local Circumstances and Practices*

Underpinning all Big *h*ART projects is a pedagogical approach to knowledge production which is collaborative, generative and localised. This approach to learning eschews the idea that external experts know best. Certainly professional expertise is important, but the starting point is somewhat different because they are invited to work *with* communities rather than *on* them. Rather than imposing top-down solutions Big *h*ART works with local resources, assets and knowledge to research local problems, issues and questions of direct relevance to communities and this occurs within a context of human relationships. This organic approach has been revitalised in recent times through place-based education which seeks to provide 'first-hand experience of local life and in the political process of understanding and shaping what happens there' (Gruenewald, 2003a, p. 620). Returning to Gruenewald's (2003a) explanation mentioned in Chapter 3, 'places teach us about how the world works and how our lives fit into the spaces we occupy. Further, places make us: As occupants of particular places with particular attributes, our identity and our possibilities are shaped' (p. 621).

Attempts to rejuvenate communities using local inquiry and artistic production are at the centre of Big *h*ART's moral endeavour to enhance 'the quality and feel of relationships between people' (Theobold, 1997, p. 121). Again, Mick's experience highlights something about the power of this deeply relational work:

> Another thing that's made a big impact on me is listening to the stories of people in the shows we put on. The DRIVE project had the biggest impact. I was doing sound for that, and when I was doing that I listened to the stories, and these affected me.

2.7 *Learning Is Collaborative, of Interest and Socially Useful*
Building on the previous point, Big *h*ART works in ways that engage young people in projects that are collaborative, of interest and socially useful. Each of the projects described in this book (LUCKY, GOLD and NGAPARTJI NGA-PARTJI) have been long-term and community-based, requiring a significant amount of time and energy to build rapport between stakeholders including local, state and federal agencies and professional workers including teachers, nurses, youth workers and council officers. Mick reflected on the collaborative and social dimension of his own learning as part of the DRIVE project: 'I learnt about others too. You've got to really put yourself aside a bit, when you work with other people. I slow myself down a bit and listen to others. It's more about listening to other people'.

Educational philosophers like John Dewey (1916/1994) acknowledge that all learning must be informed by 'a social spirit [whereby] intelligence directs ability to useful ends' (pp. 38–39). For this reason, Dewey (1916/1944) advocates 'conjoint activities in which those instructed take part, so that they may acquire a social sense of their own powers and of the materials and appliances used' (p. 40). In the process, young people are absorbed by their interest which allows them 'to be on the alert, to care about, to be attentive' to the things that really matter to them (p. 126).

3   **Conclusion**

Participants in this study like Mick reported a range of learning, from the acquisition of basic reading and writing skills, to technical skills such as sewing, painting, jewellery making, art, sound, set construction, photography and lighting, through to new-found social skills including self-confidence, public speaking, problem solving, and confidence to pursue further education and training. Above all, participants acknowledged the ways in which Big *h*ART created spaces for young people to engage in truly transformational learning that enabled them to remake their lives and identities for the better. As one participant explained, 'It was big picture learning ... they are learning with purpose'. Mapping this kind of learning through Mick's story we can identify a range of productive conditions that are conducive to young people's engagement with learning through the arts, among them: developing a capabilities approach; building relationships that are inclusive, engaging and enabling; creating dialogic spaces for identity work; interrupting dominant constructions of self and youth identity; remaking individual lives in communities of practice; and learning that is collaborative, of interest and socially useful. When these conditions are brought into existence in thoughtful ways, then we are more likely to see the development of individual and collective intellect, civic engagement and 'social spirit' for young people like Mick.

CHAPTER 8

Culture, Identity and 'Becoming Somebody': New Scripts and Possibilities

Story: I've always felt like an outsider here. (John)

John saw himself as a 'misfit' or 'outsider' who did not really belong. His participation in the GOLD project provided valuable resources with which to reinvent his identity in ways that he never imagined (e.g., being a writer, filmmaker and photographer) and in the process he became a highly valued member of the local community with particular knowledge and skills to contribute. John's experience demonstrates once again how engagement in the performance arts can create spaces in which young people feel safe and valued as they explore different ways of being and becoming in the world. John's story is a powerful reminder that cultural practices really matter, and the conditions of their production play a significant role in the ways in which meaning is produced and identities constituted. This is John's story.

Like your clothes are too tight and there's nowhere to grow.

It was Personnel Employment that sent me to Big *h*ART. I was out of school, hadn't got a job, had been expelled. I was rebellious. But I needed to survive. I needed to get a job. I remember the first time I walked into the Big *h*ART shopfront. It was night. 6 o'clock. I remember walking inside and talking to people. There was a vibe that I had never experienced before. In this city, there is a lot of judgement. It's often the first impression and then people make their mind up about you. It's a very close-minded, insular community. I've always felt like an outsider here. I was not social at all. Here, and in school, it's been like your clothes are too tight and there's nowhere to grow. But when I walked into Big *h*ART, they were friendly.

The people at Big *h*ART don't judge. The vibe was positive. I didn't have a lot of positivity to my life, so when I walked into Big *h*ART it was like a moth to a flame. Big *h*ART has attracted a lot of us misfits, the people who don't fit in. A lot of us couldn't fit into proper schooling, were expelled, left school early, had problems at home. But Big *h*ART gave us a positive environment, it allowed choice; from being a writer to being involved in film, arts, sculptures, claymation films, and that affected me. I have 70 to

© KONINKLIJKE BRILL NV, LEIDEN, 2021 | DOI: 10.1163/9789004461574_008

80 paintings. While school is a closed off environment, Big *h*ART isn't. It gave us an opportunity to grow.

It's built my confidence. I can interact with people, on multiple levels. A 180-degree change to what I used to be. Before Big *h*ART and the GOLD project, I was not a people person. But in going to the GOLD show and engaging with people regularly in a wide range of activities and projects, you just learn skills to engage with people, work together, collaborate creatively. To be a better person personally. I mean, to have a conversation like this and not feel like it's a waste of time. I'm getting something out of talking, but before Big *h*ART I wouldn't have had that. Big *h*ART allows me to think from a different perspective, and allows me to control my actions. Over time I have become a pacifist rather than getting angry and violent. It's about learning and growing into my true potential.

1   Introduction

In this chapter we focus on John's story to illuminate the kinds of cultural practices that enable identity work to occur as young people navigate the process of 'becoming somebody' (Wexler, 1992). Drawing on Paulo Freire's (1970/2000) seminal book *Pedagogy of the oppressed*, we are interested in understanding how young people develop the power 'to perceive critically *the way they exist* in the world *with which* and *in which* they find themselves; [and how] they come to see the world not as a static reality, but as a reality in process, in transformation' (p. 83). Underpinning Freire's position is the view that all young men and women are in the 'process of *becoming* – as unfinished, uncompleted beings in and with a likewise unfinished reality' (p. 84). From this standpoint, in this chapter we seek to advance a more complex and sophisticated understanding of the ways in which culture shapes identity and serves to either limit or enable new possibilities and scripts.

It was Dewey (1916/1944) at the beginning of the last century, according to Greene (2010), who argued that to be educated meant becoming different, and this might mean 'reaching towards others in a public space, achieving a community that is forever incomplete' (p. 1). Greene (2010), with a long commitment to the notion of 'incompleteness', goes on to underscore how

> the arts can move the young to see what they have never seen, to view unexpected possibilities. They are always there on the margins to refuse the indecent, the unjust, to awaken the critical and committed to visions of things being otherwise. (p. 1)

In pursuing this vision, we find Bauman's (1999) notion of 'culture as praxis' helpful because it allows us to do two things: firstly, to interrupt traditional 'sharing, agreeing and bounding' versions of culture that 'fly in the face of the facts of unequal knowledge and the differential prestige of lifestyles' and secondly, to divulge something about the 'worldviews and agency of those who are marginalized or dominated' (p. 12). As we shall see, this more dynamic version of culture opens up revitalised possibilities of 'public action' and 'equality of agency' for young people like John who are living on the margins (Rao & Walton, 2004).

Bauman (1999) expands this line of reasoning by describing the 'logical paradox' of culture, by which he means the inherent tension between the idea of culture as the activity of 'the free roaming spirit, the site of creativity, invention, self-critique, and self-transcendence' and 'culture as a tool of routinization and continuity – a handmaiden of the social order' (p. xvi). What we like about Bauman's approach is that culture is seen as much more than lifestyle or habits, routines and customs with which we have grown comfortable. Rather, it involves the persistent tensions between 'inventing/preserving' and 'change/reproduction' (p. xiv).

Viewed in this way, culture is always infused with radical possibilities because it can free 'the most daring, the least compliant and conformist spirits' who are willing to break with tradition and 'step beyond closely guarded boundaries and blaze new trails' (Bauman, 1999, p. xvi). This creative spirit informs Big *h*ART's efforts to produce high-quality artistic performances to promote public awareness, local agency and cultural change.

In the context of this more expansive view of culture, we are interested in the processes of identity formation. Identity is an elusive concept and draws on many fields of knowledge and experience, marking both place and character; it is layered with meaning that is personal, social, historical and contextual. In this sense, it is significant in participatory arts because it reflects the lives of those engaged in it and the place they grow out of. As a concept, identity has, and continues to have, explanatory power when thinking about people, for example, what is felt, culture and the contexts that shape people, whom one is, and the relationships between people and their contexts/cultures, linking both parts and wholes. However, the idea of change and a sense of self – or *becoming* – and the hope that is implicit in it, makes this domain of change an important site to consider even if there is scepticism about whether there is in effect one true or 'authentic' self to become.

Throughout this research we have used stories to describe the ways in which identity has evolved, changed or developed. For example John, whose portrait we share here, went from being someone whom people crossed the road to avoid, to someone who provided quality customer service in the job he ultimately secured. We were told that shoppers intentionally sought John out because of his knowledge and manner. This newly formed, socially accessible identity was unrecognisable to those who previously knew him.

What is key to this domain and all of the others identified throughout this broader project is that there is no one path, or lock-step form of progression within it, nor even one 'ideal' self, and of particular importance is the way identity exists in relationship to others, and how it is constantly being constructed and re-constructed in context. Consistent with participatory arts as a field of practice, this relational work reveals the centrality of the idea of sociality in Big hART's work where relationships are built, sustained and then shared through the art that is created in, with and for a community.

Key to Big hART's processes, for example, is the importance of creating art that is placed in various fora, ranging from communities of origin, no matter how small or remote, to national arts festivals or community events. This means that the way participants express whom they are is witnessed by others, thereby building, affirming or re-affirming their identity and sense of social worth.

Implicit in these processes is the importance of others. For example, whenever we think about ourselves or how we live our lives, we are reflecting questions of 'self', and how we know ourselves is profoundly influenced by comparisons we make between ourselves and others. In this understanding, it is possible to argue that there is no sense of self without other people.

In the same way, how we act is also influenced by the way others live their lives. What are 'acceptable' clothes to wear, foods to eat, and ways to live and die grow out of the culture we are embedded in or refer to, and this can be either inclusionary or exclusionary – having both negative and positive consequences. In short, how we live and how we act are complex and are interactions between a personal project of self, and how groups understand themselves.

This means that we must consider both individuals and groups, in this case community, the nested contexts in which they exist, and the way that art can meaningfully build bridges between them. In each of the arts projects described in this book, participants created work that was then viewed in the communities they came from. The art became the currency of exchange between participants and their community, and because this was of high quality, perceptions of the participants changed, in John's case from a person to be avoided at all costs to someone intentionally sought out. In the remainder of this chapter we move on to consider some of the productive practices that support these social transformations.

2   Productive Practices

In this section we identify and describe those productive practices that enabled John to transform his own sense of self from pushing back against what he saw as a 'closed' community where he was a 'misfit', to identifying himself as an artist and celebrating his own point of difference.

2.1   *Performing Identity*

Contemporary understandings of identity highlight that it is performed (Butler, 1990; Dimitriadis, 2009; Horsfall, 2008). Big *h*ART provides tools and opportunities for identity to be inquired into, experimented with – in the sense of trying on new identities – and then communicated, or rendered visible, to others. John's story, for example, reveals some of the affective dimensions of identity formation, including: (i) how participants view themselves; (ii) what they do; and (iii) the way they connect to others.

Big *h*ART provides opportunities for performing identities; in this case and consistently across projects through providing choices and creative opportunities, and support to participate in them. John, along with other young people, was provided with opportunities to be a writer, filmmaker, photographer and painter amongst other things. In his words, his experiences ranged 'from being a writer to being involved in film, arts, sculptures, claymation films, and that affected me'.

This means new and emergent roles can be engaged and experimented with through creative exploration. These opportunities were provided through workshops with artists, and were supported through mentorship with experts along with the use of high-class materials and equipment. What is significant about these opportunities was that participants' creative dispositions were strengthened and they were encouraged to act as makers. The act of making requires something of the self both as a *mediator* and *maker*, and expressing oneself in relation to others in ways traditionally not available to young people such as John. We shall have more to say about the power to create and make things shortly.

Identity, then, in this context becomes a choice, a creative selection for purposeful performance. In performing identity, the possibility of the new is embodied, allowing it to become part of an individual and collective experience and psyche, hence linking *being, belonging* and *doing* in powerful ways. Thus, performing or 'writing' a new identity is an act of agency rich with potential to create and transform; it is a 'shaping of presence' for participants, potentially enabling them to 'be' and 'be seen' differently. John's story exemplifies this. It is also clear that these arts-based practices create a 'third space' that enables participants' and others' levels of reflection and inquiry that are not normally available. In other words, 'working on' and interpreting what was made or captured for reflection enables meaning making – including what is new or unexpected – to be shared. What this means, and consistent with Jessop (2016), is that the arts can strengthen identity, enabling young people to overcome challenges and meet complex needs, and so to flourish (White, 2009).

2.2   *Making Identities*

Key to understanding the idea of a new or emergent self is the support provided by arts workers in making identities. This support ranged, for example, from pragmatic things like providing transport to workshops or events, providing food at timely points, to the sophisticated ability to know when to push for a new level of commitment towards quality, and when to hold back and provide 'space'. Making art, making time, making relationships and making things that matter were consistent principles across the three project sites. Making in this way can be understood as (re)presenting identity. In the most positive sense this allows reimagining and remapping connections to self, community and place – this is place making in the sense of finding a place as an antidote to being lost or being dislocated.

Knowing how you fit in, or not, is key to identity formation. John is a good example of those 'misfits, the people who don't fit in'. Project work enabled him to both see himself, and then be seen, differently. In John's words, 'Over time I have become a pacifist rather than getting angry and violent. It's about learning and growing into my true potential'.

2.3   *Valuing Local Knowledges*

Sadly, Indigenous young people do not always have access to their own cultural heritage or knowledge in a way that enables them to feel a sense of pride and belonging. One community member, for example, recounted: 'The project gave them the opportunity to reconnect and get to know their history through the older generation'.

Big *h*ART endeavours to move beyond a commitment to participation and inclusion to sharing new and emerging ideas or abilities that might otherwise be overlooked. For example, in each of the three projects considered for this research participants revealed stories that reflected many 'truths', making meaningful what otherwise might have remained hidden. For example, in NGAPARTJI NGAPARTJI Trevor Jamieson performed his family's story of the British atomic testing at Maralinga, presenting an insider's view and Indigenous perspective on this episode. His family story stood in stark contrast to 'official' accounts.

Young men and those who loved them in the DRIVE project – one component of LUCKY – described rites of passage, what they meant and consequences of risk. And young people, through GOLD, shared images of the ravages of insidious drought on family life in rural and regional Australia, building bridges across a divide between those who produce and those who then consume food.

In each case, participants' viewpoints offered rich readings that had been hidden or marginalised, meaning that identities were elaborated and made resonant, and in some cases cultural resources were accessed for the first time. These richer readings that were made available through the range of local artefacts produced not only enabled and animated participants and local knowledges, but also helped those around them to move beyond reductive and stigmatising views. One local council member, for example, explained: 'I used to cross over the road when I saw [this young person] coming, now we stop and chat'.

2.4   The Power to Co-Create

In the most practical way, Big hART provided creative opportunities for participation in projects with meaning and authenticity that simply would not have existed without their presence. This was particularly profound in rural and remote locations where geography, transport, facilities and expertise were limited or non-existent (Anwar McHenry, 2009). These opportunities were supported by artists who were not only skilled in their arts practice, but able to be 'in service' to others using their experience and knowledge of arts practice to support participants' own creative inquiries and expression. An adjunct to this support was not only high-quality processes, but materials and public performance or showing, thereby putting an individual's and collective's art in the world.

What the arts workers brought to each project was a sophisticated understanding of how to make art, the power of the aesthetic, and creative problem solving. More than this was a commitment to making art *with, of, for* and *in* community, meaning that it was authentic and had meaning for those who made it. As Matarasso (2019) explains, the power to create is key, that is, a deliberate act upon the world where something is brought into being, rather than a good in and of itself. The 'power to create' is broadly understood to be a process of giving form to feeling. This points to the *sensate cognition* that reflects different forms of knowledge creation and forms of inquiry and so is both aesthetic and educational in nature.

Maxine Greene (2001b), one of the most influential and prominent thinkers about the power to create, highlights three key features of aesthetic education: first, engagement with the arts heightens perception through strengthening sensate abilities, in other words a stronger sense of awareness; second, the arts ignite the imagination and so enhance creativity; and third, the arts can challenge preconceived notions though the power to see things as if they could be otherwise.

2.5   Regard, Recognition and Affect

Unconditional positive regard for others is a term usually attributed to the humanist Carl Rodgers (1980). It basically means that a person is accepted and supported regardless of their social status, level of ability or biography. It is generally accepted that this notion is important for positive human development and so has particular salience for arts workers who work with marginalised and disenfranchised groups. For example, young people often push back against what they see as attempts at paternalistic support or care. Big hART workers through this capacity for relational ways of being and working are able metaphorically to 'hold' someone as they transition to a new sense of self.

Putting it another way, changes in identity are contingent on being recognised by others. Big hART has a commitment to valuing the quality artefacts developed through creative opportunities placing them in society. These take a variety of forms and range from live theatre productions growing out of a community's own stories, to portraits (taken by participants) in a photography exhibition. This means that stereotypes of particular groups – 'at risk' young people, the elderly and so on – are challenged as audiences can literally see participants in a new light.

Building on but going beyond public performance is the 'eventness' of the work. This not only engages participants, allowing them to 'perform' differently in a public way, but affects those who bear witness to them and their experiences. This provides reciprocal benefits. There are changes of public perception and the possibility of action animated through a moral or ethical dimension. In addition, participants are allowed to belong more to the wider community who become a congregation to the work, thereby being united through the public witnessing that occurs. John explained:

> Before Big hART and the GOLD project, I was not a people person. But in going to the GOLD show and engaging with people regularly in a wide range of activities and projects, you just learn skills to engage with people, work together, collaborate creatively.

At the heart of this pedagogical transformation is the valuing of rich personal stories. This means that not only are strong feelings evoked but these are remembered in ways that resonate as familiar human feelings and human interactions, thus referencing levels of connectedness and/or disconnectedness. In tracing her own memories of returning home to Kentucky after a distinguished academic career, bell hooks (2009) provides an extraordinary insight into what it means to be more fully human in relation to people, place and culture. She draws on Carol Flinders' (2003) book *Rebalancing the world* to define a deep culture of belonging in which there is 'intimate connection with the land to which one belongs, empathetic relationship to animals, self-restraint, custodial conservation, deliberateness, balance, expressiveness, generosity, egalitarianism, mutuality, affinity for alternative modes of knowing, playfulness, inclusiveness, nonviolent conflict resolution, and openness to spirit' (2009, p. 13). Drawing on these life-affirming and humane values we can begin to see how Big *h*ART endeavours to rebuild communities through the performance arts.

3   Conclusion

We now better understand that there are many 'identities' one can have; these are not 'fixed' but are flexible and hence negotiable and, importantly for this project, jointly accomplished with – or sometimes against – others. This chapter has revealed that participatory arts is a powerful way to engage with, inquire into and express identity. Identity and culture, individual and social action, and the way that these are afforded through the arts bring collective voice and action, social justice and individuation, and cultural learning into sharper focus. As Big *h*ART's work shows, participatory arts provide multimodal forms of inquiry and expression to bear on these formative forces or lived contexts – of advantage and disadvantage – with both a level of criticality and a way of understanding the complex dynamics. This reveals ways in which participatory arts, and Big *h*ART in particular, can make a difference to those it touches through depth, inclusivity and common purpose.

Overall, Big *h*ART projects are a platform for individuals to access, explore and express their cultural identity as well as a way of experiencing other cultures. This is particularly significant because it exemplifies cultural learning, with the projects in this sense being understood as cultural pedagogies. It is also important to understand that these purposes exist within a context of cultural rights (United Nations, 1948), social and environmental degradation, and social justice. In UNESCO's words: 'At a time when artists, cultural minorities, cultural heritage and cultural expressions are increasingly under attack, defending the cultural rights of individuals and communities has never been more important' (2018, p. 1). With an understanding of pedagogy as walking alongside, Bill Ayers (2004) points out that the purpose of education is to help young people 'to become more powerfully and self-consciously alive ... to become more fully human' (p. 1). In this sense, Big *h*ART embodies a cultural pedagogy that is committed to a more expansive view of 'what we might become rather than who we are' (McLaren, 1995, p. 109). Leaving the final word to John, 'The people at Big *h*ART don't judge. The vibe was positive. I didn't have a lot of positivity to my life, so when I walked into Big *h*ART it was like a moth to a flame'.

CHAPTER 9

Culture, Arts, Justice and Activism: Lessons from the Field

In this chapter we draw together many of the multifarious threads that run through, interact, circumscribe and provide the strength to Big *h*ART's work. Set in the broader landscape of participatory arts, we have foregrounded a number of theoretical tools and empirical work, recognising that there are always a plurality of perspectives, tools for thinking with, and lenses through which we may look. In this regard we made some choices knowing that, in choosing some, we also left others out. We also clearly understand that not all projects are strong or realise their aspirations. We exist, for example, in a 'laboratory' of life where variables can not be isolated or controlled and always has a dynamic quality. The ultimate goal of the research, however, was to consider what works, for whom, when, and in what ways? As one exemplary producer, Big *h*ART provides one opportunity to develop in-depth understandings of 'what works' evidenced in the ways that participants were enabled to engage in society, connect with others, better deal with challenging life circumstances, and be heard exemplified through some of the participants themselves.

It is also important to note that each of these learnings identified in participatory projects might be broadly understood to be 'cultural solutions' that reflect 'cultural justice' in the way that both 'learnings' and 'justice' imply others and the right to thrive (Hawkes, 2001; Rankin, 2018). This broader understanding reflects the complexity within participatory arts as a form of art making that goes beyond reductive thinking that sees culture as singular, controllable and homogenous (Matarasso, 2020).

The complexity of this form of participatory arts practice where culture is both a strength and a limitation is a defining attribute, as was the complex interaction of *people, place* and *context*. Better understanding these interactions, through the different lenses this research provided, increases the potential to develop more sophisticated responses ranging from effective public policy, to practitioners gaining deeper insights into participants' needs and experiences, increasing potential for achieving positive life outcomes. We do this through highlighting particular attributes and dimensions of Big *h*ART's work, that is, how we may know it and then the richness and multilayered elements to it. We describe four defining attributes: disadvantage, a processual approach, creativity, and four pillars of support. Second, we describe seven 'domains of change'

© KONINKLIJKE BRILL NV, LEIDEN, 2021 | DOI: 10.1163/9789004461574_009

or areas where change and transformation were visible: health and wellbeing; building community; agency; an expressive life; productive lives; learning; and identity.

Next we highlight the 20 productive conditions and practices that enable change to be *informed, enacted* and *sustained* into transformation over time. This chapter links the practice knowledge developed from the field with the theoretical thinking described in the preceding chapters.

1   Attributes and Dimensions

During this project we have considered three significant Big *h*ART projects – LUCKY, NGAPARTJI NGAPARTJI and GOLD. They were significant in the way that they covered different locations including rural and remote, worked with different groups of participants, were multi-generational and diverse by culture, and addressed different needs: juvenile justice, deaths in custody, discrimination, invisibility, binge drinking and autocide[1] for example. While each was distinct in a number of different ways, they also shared much in common, not the least the way that each was multilayered, rich with different textual elements, and with different dimensions.

While the projects occurred in disparate parts of Australia, across three different states and territories (Tasmania, New South Wales and the Northern Territory), they shared some common attributes that are representative of participatory arts in general (Finkelpearl, 2014; Lewis, 2013; Matarasso, 2019), and Big *h*ART in particular. Of these attributes, the first and most important is the way that this form of socially engaged art involves working with a 'wicked problem' (Rittel & Webber, 1973) identified by the community itself. The processes of art making with these communities are then both ways to investigate the issue itself, and to express the outcomes of that process through high-quality art in public spaces. Helguera describes this as a 'space of ambiguity' where the 'realm of art-making ... brings new insights to a particular problem or condition and in turn makes it visible' (2011, p. 5). Through this process Big *h*ART is politically active and works towards social change. Of the range of features engaged with across these projects, four are key.

1.1   *Disadvantage*
All communities that Big *h*ART works in are circumscribed by characteristics of disadvantage, where disadvantage can be understood in several ways. In Tasmania, for example, this included young people who are marginalised and disenfranchised, as well as older people who are on the margins without

social support. In New South Wales, it included young people disengaged from community and leading lives that are often discounted in the economic rationalist master story of our times, and so perceived as 'costs' to society rather than 'benefits'. And in the Northern Territory, Big *h*ART worked with Indigenous Australians, who as the first Australians are struggling to reclaim and reaffirm their identity in the context of colonialism, poor living conditions and life circumstances often beyond their control – this being at odds with Australia's status as an economically developed country with a good social support system. These First Nations people are negatively portrayed by the media and racist groups as being 'helpless' and' hopeless', but this is simply racism at its worst. What the research revealed, for example, is fertile veins of culture that are accessed and strengthened through arts practice across each site, and that are also evolving and rich with possibility.

In each site, Big *h*ART worked *with* the community, *in* the community, *from* the community, and *for* the community. This multivalent approach could be understood as being in service to the community, and so honouring the issues each particular community saw as important, rather than Big *h*ART deciding in advance what each project might be. More formally this approach is both participatory in nature and also evidences democracy at work (Graves, 2005), foregrounding 'cultural democracy' in particular (Adams & Goldbard, 1995; Thomson, Hall, Earl, & Geppert, 2019).

1.2 *A Processual Approach*

Each of the projects followed a similar trajectory that could be understood to occur in six separate phases. In phase one extensive *consultation* occurred. This could be simply described as a process of *deep listening* (Butterwick & Selman, 2003). In phase two, *opportunities* for engagement were provided through the provision of extensive consultation and workshops. A key feature of these processes is the 'power of the personal'. What this means is that, once there were some initial project participants, these participants used their personal networks and contacts to draw in others; this process is similar to 'snowballing' used in research methodology (Seidman, 2013). Through engagement came *participation*. Although engagement and participation are talked about separately, the two are intrinsically linked. For example, we were able to see that personal networks led to new participants attending workshops. And in addition, through participation in the workshops engagement with, and then contributions to, the project developed relationally. However, this participation with, contributions towards, and ultimately ownership of the project – developed through arts practice – would not occur without engagement in the first place.

In phase four, *skills* were taught and developed through the workshop format. Individuals and groups were given skills not only to develop new knowledge and capacities through arts practice, including knowledge of self and cultural knowledges, but also the social skills necessary for these to be applied in a group context. In phase five, as a result of skills developed and practised, *expertise* was developed and employed, leading to phase six, *expression*. In this phase project participants' skills were employed to 'make' artefacts that were placed in the community and other public fora; in other words, participants 'worked as' artists. This had the consequence for participants of developing pride, having their experience 'witnessed', and hence the opportunity to develop both bridging and bonding forms of social capital (Patulny & Svendsen, 2007). This included the norms of respect and trust available by acting across formal gradients of power or authority that Szreter and Woolcock (2004) describe as 'linking' social capital. Also, more particularly, community life and culture were enriched through the sharing of meaning and experience that was also contained in and expressed through art (Sharpe, 2010; Wright & Pascoe, 2015), creating dialogic spaces.

1.3   *Creativity as an Essential Element of Healthy Community*
In each project Big *h*ART seeks to tackle social disadvantage through actively involving people in 'creative expressions of their life and identity within cultural and arts practice', thereby building social cohesion and productive, healthy, self-supporting futures through networked structures. This approach follows a socially inclusive, asset-based community development model that focuses not on deficits or a welfare model, but rather on the strengths and skills already present but unacknowledged in the respective communities, in this way seeking to develop and build on these qualities (Bungay & Clift, 2010; Kay, 2000).

1.4   *Four Pillars of Support*
Big *h*ART's commitment towards social change is built on four related but separate pillars of support, working simultaneously with individuals, communities, nations and arts fora, and highlighting both vertical and horizontal planes of connection.

1.4.1   Individuals: Building Social and Economic Participation
In the creative workshops, for example, genuine interest is taken in the participants' stories, personalities and development, promoting an atmosphere of mutual respect. These workshops do not require any particular skills from the participants to begin with. They are designed to experiment with different art

forms in order to find an appropriate medium for individuals to express their own story.

In this process, strong personal relationships with participants are built and individuals are also linked with professional artists and cultural workers across a wide range of creative workshops incorporating different forms. In the context of this relational work, facilitating exchange between participants from different walks of life but with similar experiences of marginalisation helps to dismantle stereotypes, promotes empathy, and situates individual experience in a social context, lessening feelings of isolation and re-engaging people with their community. This generative process, building from individuals to small groups, is bridging, bonding and linking.

In addition, the small group workshop focus (building if necessary from a one-on-one mentoring process) facilitates an artistic exchange of personal stories, their meaning, and how they can be translated into high-quality art while encouraging individuals to expand their social and professional skills in a supportive environment. This relational work is key to achieving high levels of engagement and maintaining artistic excellence.

This approach is grounded in the belief that every daily act contributes to the constant construction of personal identity and that imagination is essential to this basic selfhood narrative. It allows for critical perspectives on choices and trying out new models of living, opening up alternative pathways while equipping the individual with purposefulness to organise his or her life and relationships in healthy ways.

1.4.2 Communities: Building Connections and Capacity for Change

To amplify the influence of its projects and to enable sustained change in the community, Big hART actively seeks to form partnerships with local institutions, organisations, individuals and government bodies. Exchange of knowledge and the development of an arts- and culture-based model of sustained community development are key objectives for these partnerships. This means that, when quality artwork is presented to the general community, participants experience a positive form of attention and appreciation. For example, performance creates a communicative environment and challenges audiences to reflect on preconceived ideas relating to the persons involved who have previously been relegated to the margins of the community (Goldbard, 2017).

In performative terms, when audiences see 'everyday life' performed as art – in other words 'made special' – they are invited to identify with the narrations of 'the other'. This arts practice provides literal and metaphorical space for an individual to belong amid the community. We understand this to be a 'third space' which is in between the individual and the community – a space

that is animated through art that also amplifies the influence of the project
and enables sustained change in the community (Goldbard, 2013; Leonard &
Kilkelly, 2006; Tulloch, 1999).

1.4.3   Nation: Contributing to Social Policy Change

Presenting high-quality artwork to a wider, national audience in mainstream
venues offers a new domain of experience to participants, while at the same
time raising awareness of issues facing disadvantaged communities. Big *h*ART
then uses this awareness and public profile in the political domain to push for
policy changes that will support the community to tackle its problems and create follow-on effects for other communities facing similar issues. One powerful
example of these effects is Big *h*ART's direct influence on the development of
a national Indigenous languages policy (Sometimes & Kelly, 2010), as well as
contributions towards policy developments on domestic violence and crime
prevention (Wright, 2009, 2012; Wright & Palmer, 2007).

1.4.4   Art: Creating Exquisite, High-Calibre Art Outcomes for National
and International Festivals

Creating art lies at the heart of Big *h*ART's work. It is a tripartite approach: first,
a process of enquiry for participants, where issues related to their *being* in the
world can be inquired into; second, a means of upskilling participants in arts-
specific skills and knowledge, providing them with both *specific* and *general*
expressive and arts-related skills that are task specific and also transferable,
strengthening, for example, creative dispositions and capabilities; and third, a
form of expression that leads to recognition of aesthetic outcomes, endowing
the project and participants with status and recognition.

More specifically, in the last 15 years Big *h*ART has presented 18 major professional works, including highly acclaimed films, performances and artworks,
in over 12 Australian and international festivals. This process in turn not only
builds pride and respect for participants and communities, but also develops
what Stam refers to as 'witnessing publics', who are 'loose collection of individuals, constituted by and through the media, acting as observers of injustices
that might otherwise go unreported or unanswered' (2015, p. 282).

Underscoring the importance of this approach, Cohen-Cruz also notes that
art is only useful for those involved in political activism and social change if it
'convinces, challenges or inspires the audience in particular ways' (2010, p. 45),
and for this to happen there needs to be 'aesthetic strategies that are compelling'
(p. 95). Big *h*ART embodies these processes with high-quality art that creates
openings to understand how others' lived experience is shaped and embodied.

Next we turn our attention to those areas where social change might be
visible.

2   Evidence of Change

One important element of this research was to highlight areas where we might usefully look for evidence of change and the personal experiential forms of knowledge that are important for practice (Nutley, Powell, & Davies, 2013). We are also mindful that 'evidence of change' is a tension debated across different forms of inquiry including arts-based work and differing forms of development (Lennie & Tacchi, 2013; Morse, Swanson, & Kuzel, 2001) in the zeitgeist of accountability (Donaldson, Christie, & Melvin, 2009). These debates include arguments for the abandonment of the concept of data itself (Ellingson & Sotirin, 2019).

It has also been our experience that what constitutes evidence varies, that there is a current fetish for metrification, and that 'proof' of change in and of itself means very little for practice. One stark difference in understanding 'what counts' is the differentiation between experience-near and experience-distant – or micro versus macro – perspectives (Huss & Bos, 2019) and what each perspective privileges (Froggett & Briggs, 2012). For Big hART's participants and arts workers what counts directly relates to their lived experience that is experiential, sensate and subjective, whereas those who view the work from a distance look for disembodied, aggregated and abstracted counting mechanisms. This means that there can often be a mismatch between expectations and evidence and the imposition of regimes of measurement developed for laboratories and bio-medical fields rather than a focus on the embodied, affective and aesthetic – the lived experience in other words.

Our preference is the view that there is less utility value in answering questions about causality, and more in answering 'why?' and 'in what ways?' questions. More specifically: What works for whom? In what ways, and circumstances? And for whose benefit? (Pawson & Tilley, 1997). These key questions point to the way that participatory arts generally, and Big hART specifically, work in 'complex systems' (Preskill & Gopal, 2014) in creative ways beyond inputs, outputs, linearity and lock-step progression. The following sections highlight how we might better address such questions with a view to improving practice rather than simply 'proving' that it works.

3   Domains of Change

Through this research we have been able to describe seven domains of change. We have intentionally not named these domains 'indicators', as the term is often used in a reductive way and indicates a singular point to be reached. This mechanistic logic implies a form of step-wise or lockstep development – and hence, an end to meet in itself – that makes no sense in participatory arts practice where the social, relational and aesthetic interact in dynamic ways. It is clear to us that disaggregation of practice into discrete factors and variables, to use the formal language of monitoring and evaluation, is blind to the complicated nature of human change and development, the ecology of arts practice as the dynamic field in which change sits, and the palette of possibilities that facilitate it. In participatory arts practice change is *both* the *means* and the *ends* where benefits accrue.

Consequently we have used the language of 'domains' of change. A domain follows a different logic that we think of as a broad area with porous rather than hard boundaries, not a singular discrete silo, recognising that participants both enter and leave projects at different points, with different experiences, proclivities, needs and aspirations. A domain of change, as it is used in the development field (Dart & Davies, 2003), is rather a 'place to look', or even a signpost pointing the way. This means that, if change is to occur through project involvement, then it could be apparent across *any one* of the domains or *combinations* of these. These domains are purposefully broad as it is possible that individuals experience them differently. Nevertheless domains serve as useful conceptual organisers when looking at Big *h*ART's work.

Key to this understanding is that these domains are not mutually exclusive, and that they exist in association with each other. For example, as young people develop agency, they are more likely to experience wellbeing and move towards work of meaning and value. Our research reveals that there are many paths to change, and in this complex dynamic these domains by themselves might be necessary, but not necessarily sufficient for change in and of themselves. We now turn our attention to these domains of change.

3.1   *Enhancing Health and Wellbeing through Networks and Relationships*

This domain foregrounds the psychosocial processes that need to be generated to positively influence an individual's thoughts and resulting behaviours. The focus is on understanding how participants develop psychologically as they interact in the Big *h*ART social-aesthetic environment. Psychosocial processes help people become more mentally healthy via self-expression, perspective (the comparison of self to others and therefore seeing things differently), self-determination (the option to choose what they would like to do rather than being told), and building a sense of efficacy, confidence, positive self-image, resilience and belonging. These outcomes are strongly linked in well-established research on arts and health (Mowlah, Niblett, Blackburn, & Harris, 2014).

Reflected in this domain is the unique manner in which Big *h*ART is able to work with participants, artists, funders and the community to enhance the psychosocial wellbeing of people involved in its projects. Also of significance is the way Big *h*ART projects show participants there are options and opportunities available to them by strengthening their capabilities and capacities. In addition, Big *h*ART makes participants feel secure by creating friendly and safe places to work, with people who care about participant wellbeing, who do not judge, and will support participants to achieve their aspirations.

Across the three sites, participants, artists, community members and funders acknowledged the benefits of engaging in projects such as LUCKY, NGAPARTJI NGAPARTJI and GOLD. In relation to health and wellbeing, participants moved from a situation of disconnection to community re-connection by expanding their network of friends and acquaintances, creating positive peer relationships, interacting with artist and community mentors, participating more fully in their community and 'escaping' their everyday lives. According to participants, Big *h*ART had a positive impact on their life by increasing their:

- confidence
- self-esteem/self-worth
- self-image/self-pride
- hope for the future
- motivation.

Participants also shared that their participation in a Big *h*ART project led to feelings of:

- happiness
- achievement
- enjoyment
- excitement
- enthusiasm
- belonging
- acceptance
- empowerment.

Each of these were key to participants' psychosocial and emotional development. In addition, in a trans-dimensional way, Big *h*ART projects improved participants' knowledge and skills (arts, expression, communication and associated multi-literacy skills), reduced feelings of isolation and reinforced to participants that each was important, highlighting the role of the arts in social inclusion (Jensen, Stickley, & Edgley, 2016; Swan, 2013; White, 2004).

3.2 *Building Communities through Creative Spaces*

This domain points to the cultural and artistic processes created and sustained in order to build a sense of community, or interdependence between people within a particular place and space. The focus is on understanding how people, often from diverse backgrounds including gender, age, race, class and location, come together to enhance the quality and feel of the relationships between them. Of particular interest is the manner in which collaborative artistic performances can assist communities in the task of enhancing intergenerational relationships, developing a spirit of reciprocity, and preserving local funds of knowledge (Gonzalez et al., 2006) including oral histories, memories and cultural artefacts.

Put another way, this domain points to evidence of participants mobilised through the human, social, cultural and economic resources necessary to build a spirit of community through creative performance. Participants, for example, become part of communities of practice that enable them to develop a sense of connectedness and feelings of belonging to place (Schneekloth & Shibley, 1995; Wenger, 1998; Wright & Palmer, 2007). In these times of economic and social insecurity where the values of individualism, consumerism, competitiveness and materialism control all aspects of our lives, there is an urgent need to reinvigorate the role of communities as the cornerstone of human affairs.

In highlighting this domain, we heard over and over again from participants about the benefits of engaging in projects such as LUCKY, NGAPARTJI NGAPARTJI and GOLD in terms of generating cultural and social meaning for individuals and communities alike. The LUCKY project in Tasmania identified struggling teenage mothers and their children, elderly people living in isolated circumstances, and young men at risk of harm as communal concerns. In the GOLD project in the Murray-Darling Basin the focus was on crime prevention and community development by engaging with marginalised youth and farming families devastated both emotionally and financially by the impact of climate change, extended periods of drought and severe water shortages.

The NGAPARTJI NGAPARTJI arts-based community development and language project conducted with Indigenous people across the Anangu, Pitjantjatjara and Yankunytjatjara (APY) Lands in Central Australia addressed the damaging fallout caused by the forcible removal of Indigenous peoples from their land after the Second World War by preserving the community's language, art, cultural knowledge and social cohesion.

Thus, when we look closely at the narratives of participants we see emerging evidence of positive impacts on:

– intergenerational engagement and connection
– quantity and quality of relationships
– sense of belonging and connectedness

- peer and family relationships
- collaboration among community members and stakeholders
- awareness of community assets and resources
- civic engagement and spirit of generosity.

Noting that each domain is not a silo, we also saw evidence that participants were developing new skills, capabilities and dispositions not only to see the world differently and more optimistically, but to challenge some damaging stereotypes, attitudes and behaviours in more productive and creative ways.

3.3   Developing Agency and a Sense of Efficacy

This domain relates to a person's sense of agency, of being able to act upon the world. At its best, the notion of agency – also known as self-efficacy – encompasses being confident and purposeful, and acting to direct one's life (Bandura, 1997; Moorfield-Lang, 2010). The notion of agency foregrounds individual choice, freedom and intentionality; it speaks to being purposeful and the benefits that flow including having and taking control in one's life.

This notion of agency can be understood by way of contrast to people who are passive, or have a self-image that invites abuse or manipulation, or the disempowering belief that they should 'give up'. In other words, a lack of agency results in people feeling small, worthless and inadequate, with no capacity to change or affect anything in their future; these feelings are described as 'learned helplessness' in psychological terms.

Key to understanding this domain is recognising how learned helplessness with associated feelings of powerlessness, hopelessness and an inability to change goes beyond psychology and into social action. It is also important to understand that, while behavioural change can be thought of as individual, and based on logic and rational choice, this domain reveals that behavioural change grows out of Big hART's practices of community, social acceptance, and experiences borne of deep engagement in heartfelt dialogue, creative acts, expression and reflection. In this sense, it is more than simply 'knowing' the facts, but for participants reflects 'beings and doings' that have meaning and value. It is also important to understand that each of these 'beings and doings' and what constitutes meaning and value are culturally bound.

Through Big hART's projects, and the cultural solutions that they afford, participants are able to be active and feel like they have agency, thereby building confidence and leading to transfer into other aspects of participants' lives. Consequently, while motivation to change comes from within, it is profoundly affected by the company of others and the feelings that are engendered. Hence, it is possible to look at this domain for evidence of impact of participatory arts projects, for example participants moving from self-limiting or self-compromising behaviours to those that are self-enhancing and self-affirming.

Simply put, a creative act is an act of agency rich with possibility that moves beyond directed or duplicated activity that reproduces what is taken as given. So while behavioural change, or doing something differently, is evidence of change, the process of change grows from feelings and the actions that flow from them. What this means is that we might look for how someone does something differently as evidence of impact of a Big *h*ART project through their mastery of a new skill, emulating positive role models including the arts workers and artists themselves, the development of confidence and self-belief, and the ability to persist – simply put, 'capacity in action'.

In summary, this domain encompasses change reflected through participants:
– being active
– working as artists and makers
– feeling confident
– developing self-respect
– having a positive outlook
– developing persistence.

3.4   *Using Participatory Arts for an Expressive Life*

This domain relates to the impact Big *h*ART's creative processes and artistic outcomes have on young people and their communities. From the outset it is essential to recognise that art making and producing, in its various forms and activities, lies at the centre of Big *h*ART's approach and it is impossible to separate their theatre productions and artistic products from the community engagement strategies employed to produce them. In ways which surprise many observers, their work refuses to be easily categorised into the 'neat' binaries which for so long have confounded ways of understanding art, culture and community.

Big *h*ART's work is neither 'high' art nor 'low' art, 'art for art's sake' nor popular culture or a manifestation of the intrinsic value in art over the instrumental application of art for social justice. Indeed all of these categories can be seen in aspects of their work over time, but slips and flows across and between categories produce outcomes which go beyond simplistic binary understandings to create fresh and often unnamed species of creative work. However, the abiding commitment to making art with a rich aesthetic and affective dimension is unwavering and acts as a magnetic north guiding every journey Big *h*ART makes with a community.

Linking these two key ideas of aesthetics and the social is the original meaning of aesthetics, namely perception by the senses. Qualities that are *felt* can be thought of as 'those-that-call-forth-action' (Martin, 2011), and so social-aesthetic in nature.

Reflecting this core domain, we saw evidence of impact reflected in:
- engagement in workshops (composing, acting, singing, dancing)
- engaging, participating and then contributing in workshops
- performing in theatrical and musical creations
- creating high-quality aesthetic artefacts
- developing confidence to have a voice
- speaking across cultural barriers
- feeling empowered.

3.5 Constructing Productive Lives: Aspirations and Work of Value and Meaning

This domain points to an alternative set of possibilities made available through creative practices rethinking the links between the economy and job opportunities for young people. At heart, this involves looking at individual troubles (e.g. unemployment) in relation to key economic, political and social institutions of society, and not merely the personal situation and character of individuals. It is clear that Big *h*ART enables participants to build the capabilities needed to pursue the kinds of imagined futures (dreams, aspirations, needs and desires) they identify and want to lead. This can be understood as a manifestation of Amartya Sen's (1992) capabilities through assisting young people to: (i) identify the kind of lives they want to lead; (ii) develop the skills and knowledge to do that; and (iii) understand and confront how their political, social and economic conditions enable or constrain them.

By way of summary, there is evidence that Big *h*ART's work has positive economic impacts in terms of:
- making things of interest to sell, thus building entrepreneurial spirit
- enrolling in further education and training courses to enhance skills
- developing employability skills, for example, public speaking, confidence, teamwork, creativity, and organisational and planning skills
- enhancing writing and literacy skills
- developing social networks and support structures
- developing motivation and drive.

3.6 Strengthening Capacities and Dispositions for Learning

This domain points to the ways Big *h*ART processes enhance participants' learning in terms of capabilities, knowledge and life skills. It is important to note that Big *h*ART typically works with young people who are disengaged and alienated from mainstream educational institutions such as schools, TAFE or other formal places of learning. This is important because school, for many, is not a site where the spirit can be creative and formal education often does not provide adequate support and opportunities to acquire the competencies needed for future work (Karlgren et al., 2020).

This domain highlights that Big hART creates alternative spaces where young people have an opportunity to re-engage in learning and community life through arts-based projects that are highly processual. More specifically, this domain evidences a wide range of learning, including the acquisition of fundamental life skills including improved social skills, decision making, problem solving, self-confidence and public speaking. In addition, linking across domains in a transdisciplinary way, we saw evidence of the development of basic reading and writing skills, technical skills such as sewing, painting, jewellery making, art, sound, set construction, photography and lighting, and information technology such as audio visual, camera, sound, editing and so on – each of these based on experiential workshop approaches that bring arts and learning together in educative ways (Rasmussen & Wright, 2001). This learning ultimately led to confidence to pursue further education and training and to imagine new identities and futures.

By way of summary, there is evidence of positive impacts in terms of:
– exploring future educational options
– developing confidence to speak publicly
– developing organisational and planning skills
– arts-based and arts-associated skills
– problem solving and teamwork
– writing and literacy skills
– developing social skills
– pursuing passions and interests, and
– developing a sense of self-efficacy.

3.7   (Re)inventing Identity through Cultural Practices

In this domain it is possible to see how *identity, cultural learning* and *becoming* are 'sites' of evidence when looking for impact of Big hART's work. On a cautionary note, each of these concepts are so broad that it becomes challenging to see what we might look for in practice. Identity, for example, is an elusive concept and draws on many fields of knowledge and experience, marking both place (the central desert to regional Australia) and character (Indigenous to white Australian); it is layered with meaning that is personal, social, historical and contextual. In addition, there seem to be conflicting layers of evidence. In this domain, for example, we saw how one young person transformed from someone who was avoided, people crossing the street if they saw him walking towards them, to someone who was intentionally sought out as he was inducted into and maintained a customer-service role. This reflected acceptance and welcoming by his broader community. By way of contrast, another young person with a disability began to identify as an artist and has gone on to work semi-professionally. In this case, his point of difference was celebrated and accepted, leading to an evolving identity as a musician.

In each of these two exemplars the change induced through various forms of cultural learning became transformational: the participant grew into a different state of being, from rejection to acceptance for example, both at an individual and community level. This foregrounds the importance of social aesthetics based on dialogue and exchange, including 'for what and to whom art communicates' and pointing towards change situated in particular social and physical contexts (Nielsen, 2015).

We now better understand that there are many 'identities' one can have; these are not 'fixed' but are flexible and hence negotiable and, importantly for this domain, jointly accomplished with – or sometimes against – others (Wright, 2020). More specifically, we saw evidence of participants:

- moving from exclusion to inclusion
- moving from rejecting their cultural heritage to accepting, identifying and affirming this legacy
- being active as makers within a culture rather than being 'receivers' of it, and in wider ways
- understanding identity as pluralistic, rather than singular, and identifying possibilities for difference.

4   Productive Conditions and Practices

It is clear that the work of Big *h*ART and similar participatory arts companies is complex and layered. The results of the work accrue over time and in multiple ways; put differently, there are many trajectories through it and beneficial outcomes. Drawing across all seven domains identified from the research, we are able to describe the productive conditions that support Big *h*ART's award-winning work through the practices they engender developed from over 25 years of trial and error.

We have identified 20 conditions and practices, set out below. More than just a loose set of associations that are permissive in nature, these conditions and practices allow for divergence across projects, but also are critical in producing work that counts. Importantly, these conditions are not causal in nature, but through their presence and the practices they support high-quality work emerges that is co-emergent and concomitant. In this sense they both allow for change – the possibilities inherent in creative work – and also provide an understanding of congruence across participatory arts-based work.

Put differently, what follows is the values and guiding principles that both inform and sustain the work over time, that is, the beliefs held and the qualities that surround them, and then the practices that embody and make them visible and sustained. In Big *h*ART's work, and reflective of participatory arts more generally, we see high-quality practice:

Informed by the following values and principles:
1   values that promote *individual and social growth*
2   values of *inclusiveness and respect*
3   *asset-based* rather than deficit thinking
4   *humanistic* principles
5   *relational* in nature
6   being *grounded* in community

Enacted through:
7   provision of *opportunities*
8   provision of *resources* – including financial, physical, material, and varying forms of knowledge and expertise located in arts workers, creative producers and partners
9   *embodiment* of social justice principles
10   a focus on *identity* work – individual and community
11   *creative workshops* that have meaning and authenticity
12   animation of the *imagination*
13   actively *teaching* skills that are engaging to participants
14   *support* – notions of 'holding' participants as they grow and change
15   a focus on *innovation and risk taking*, stretching participants beyond what has been taken for granted

Sustained through:
16   collaborative community partnerships
17   projects that are socially worthwhile to those who are in them, see them or might be touched by them
18   projects that culminate in a public event with the artefacts developed strategically placed in community
19   a developmental approach
20   quality in both process and product.

In overview, opportunities are provided that have certain characteristics. These opportunities foreground (but are not limited to) experience in art making that is supported through high levels of social skills and interactions, with a consequence being recognition by others. In addition, these opportunities are infused by humanitarian values and principles, the facilitation of others, and the behaviours elicited grounded in relational forms of art making or, put more simply, participants working as artists.

Finally, there are key moments within this social-aesthetic frame that are important for change to occur. In other words, art making and learning combine to teach and animate through story, providing potential for social change and transformation. Using film, documentary, theatre, arts events, and more recently podcasts, apps, digital media and augmented and virtual reality, Big *h*ART provides perspectives and insights that lead to different ways of being in the world. These insights provide a call to action with an ethical or moral dimension for participants and audiences alike.

5   Concluding Thoughts: Participatory Arts, Agency and
        Connected Belonging

We opened this book by highlighting four main purposes. First, we aimed to draw attention to the possibility of *reinvigorating communities* through participatory arts by focusing on three key issues: diversity, inclusion and equity. Our second purpose was considering how participatory arts can enable *reinventing youth identities* through interrupting deficit thinking, creating sustaining relational spaces, and promoting health and wellbeing. Third, we aimed to describe the conditions for *re-imagining alternative futures* where project participants and those around them can broaden horizons and understandings, identify possibilities, and pursue the common good through creative and cultural learnings. And the fourth purpose was *fostering activist and socially just research* through listening to young people, developing research approaches that are inclusive and respectful of the lives of the most marginalised, and reconceptualising what 'counts' as evidence. Each of these four imperatives was informed by a desire to work towards cultural justice.

Through a context of escalating change, disequilibrium, challenge and the ways in which these impact on the most vulnerable and least resourced, we looked closely at the work of Big *h*ART as one Australian producer of high-quality participatory arts practice. Spread across three separate projects, each running across a minimum of 150 weeks of engagement, and in a wide range of rural, regional and remote settings, we identified seven broad domains of change where we were able to observe change and transformation occurring. In doing this we further distilled 20 productive conditions, practices and possibilities that were enablers and helped to make clear the attributes and dimensions of such multidimensional practice. We then brought to bear a number of theoretical tools that helped us interrogate, think more deeply, and then better understand this field as it continues to emerge.

Linking each of these dimensions is the singular animating power of developing a sense of *agency to create and re-create the world*, fostered by participation that is dynamic, contingent and aesthetic. Consistent across each of these projects considered in this volume, and within the field of participatory arts more generally is the outcome of *connected belonging and solidarity*. These outcomes are always emergent, and occur through the diversity of arts practice we have highlighted. It is these shared experiences that occur through these creative and expressive processes that are both the process and product of participatory arts works. In these contexts the participatory arts provide both a means and a site of 'action', and a state of liminality or transitional space 'betwixt and between' where the new can emerge. In the confluence of these states feelings of belonging, often deeply felt, are shared, thus developing communitas (Turner, 2012). Participants described these experiences of 'making' in and with community, which, though sometimes temporary, are linked to a stronger sense of self-awareness, relational ability and a collectively felt sense of new possibilities.

This composite of sensory and cognitive dimensions of being and awareness highlight that, through action that is somaesthetic (Shusterman, 2004), the qualities of art as experience (Dewey, 1934/1959) are as apt today as ever. These qualities include connections, active engagement, sensory experience, perceptivity, risk taking and imagination. The combination of humanism and shared meaning making that lies at the heart of Big *h*ART's work means that the individual shared are relatable to sets of common experiences. These stories of young people's experiences show how participatory arts provide benefits and enrich the lives of participants, arts workers, funders and then the nation at large.

Developing the capacity for co-creation, connected belonging, and participatory arts practices that are creative and imaginative expands our understanding, empathy and respect, building new shared visions of growth and social change. In the words of Freire: 'Knowledge emerges only through invention and re-invention, through the restless, impatient, continuing, hopeful inquiry human beings pursue in the world, with the world, and with each other' (1970/2000, p. 72).

With hope for extending this future horizon, where participants can be not just in the world, but for the world, we conclude with the words of Brian Eno: 'What is possible in art, becomes thinkable in life' (1995).

Note

1   Autocide is young men attempting to self-harm through single occupant car smashes.

References

ABC News. (2018, June 7). Insecure work the 'new norm' as full-time job rate hits record low: Report. *ABC News*. Retrieved from http://www/abc.net.au/news/2018-06-07/full-time-job-rate-hits-new-low-as-casual-work-taks-over-rpeort/9840064

Adams, D., & Goldbard, A. (1995). *Cultural democracy: Introduction to an idea*. Retrieved from http://www.wwcd.org/cd2.html

Adamson, P. (2010). *The children left behind: A league table of inequality in child wellbeing in the world's rich countries* (inreca619). Florence, Italy: Innocenti Research Centre, UNICEF. Retrieved from ideas.repec.org/p/ucf/inreca/inreca619.html

Agger, B. (2004). *Speeding up fast capitalism: Culture, jobs, families, schools and bodies*. Boulder, CO: Paradigm.

Akom, A. (2007). Free spaces: Excavating race, class, and gender among urban schools and communities. *International Journal of Qualitative Studies in Education, 20*(6), 611–616.

Alexander, B. K., Anderson, G. L., & Gallegos, B. P. (Eds.). (2005). *Performance theories in education: Power, pedagogy, and the politics of identity*. Mahwah, NJ: Erlbaum Associates.

All-Party Parliamentary Group on Arts, Health and Wellbeing. (2017). *Creative health: The arts for health and wellbeing*. London, UK: All-Party Parliamentary Group on Arts, Health and Wellbeing. Retrieved from https://www.culturehealthandwellbeing.org.uk/appg-inquiry/Publications/Creative_Health_Inquiry_Report_2017_-_Second_Edition.pdf

Anwar McHenry, J. (2009). My art has a secret mission: The role of the arts in Australian rural, remote and Indigenous communities. *International Journal of the Arts in Society, 4*(1), 157–170.

Appadurai, A. (2004). The capacity to aspire: Culture and the terms of recognition. In V. Rao & M. Walton (Eds.), *Culture and public action* (pp. 59–84). Stanford, CA: Stanford University Press.

Arendt, H. (1961). *Between past and future*. New York, NY: Viking Penguin.

Arendt, H. (1990). *On revolution*. Harmondsworth, UK: Penguin.

Aronowitz, S., & DiFazio, W. (2010). *The jobless future* (2nd ed.). Minneapolis, MN: University of Minnesota Press.

Ayers, W. (2004). *Teaching toward freedom: Moral commitment and ethical action in the classroom*. Boston, MA: Beacon Press.

Bandura, A. (1986). *Social foundations of thought and action: A social cognitive theory*. Englewood Cliffs, NJ: Prentice Hall.

Bandura, A. (1997). *Self-efficacy: The exercise of control*. New York, NY: W.H. Freeman.

Barenboim, P., & Sidiqi, N. (2010). *Bruges, the bridge between civilizations: To the 75th anniversary of the Roerich Pact.* Moscow, Russia: Letny Sad.

Bauman, Z. (1999). *Culture as praxis.* London, UK: Sage.

Bauman, Z. (2002). *Society under siege.* Cambridge, UK: Polity Press.

Bauman, Z. (2004). *Wasted lives: Modernity and its outcasts.* Cambridge, UK: Polity Press.

Bauman, Z. (2011). *Collateral damage: Social inequalities in a global age.* Cambridge, UK: Polity Press.

Beadle, S., Holdsworth, R., & Wyn, J. (Eds.). (2010). *For we are young and ...? Young people in a time of uncertainty.* Carlton, Vic: Melbourne University Press.

Berlin, I. (1969). Two concepts of liberty. In I. Berlin (Ed.), *Four essays on liberty* (pp. 118–172). Oxford, UK: Oxford University Press.

Bessant, J. (2018, September 29). The future of work will not be full-time. *The Age.* Retrieved from https://www.theage.com.au/national/the-future-of-work-will-not-be-full-time-20180925-p505t5.html

Blyth, M. (2013). *Austerity: The history of a dangerous idea.* Oxford, UK: Oxford University Press.

Bourdieu, P. (1986). *Distinction: A social critique of the judgement of taste* (R. Nice, Trans.). Cambridge, MA: Harvard University Press.

Bourdieu, P. (1993). *The field of cultural production.* Cambridge, UK: Polity.

Bourdieu, P. (1998). *Acts of resistance: Against the new myths of our time.* Oxford, UK: Polity Press.

Bourriaud, N. (2002). *Relational aesthetics* (S. Pleasance & F. Woods, Trans.). Dijon, France: Les Presses du Reel.

Bowring, F. (2015). Negative and positive freedom: Lessons from, and to, sociology. *Sociology, 49*(1), 156–171.

Brendtro, L., & du Toit, L. (2005). *Response ability pathways: Restoring bonds of respect.* Claremont, South Africa: Pretext Publishers.

Bresler, L. (2004). *Knowing bodies, moving minds: Towards embodied teaching and learning.* Dordrecht, the Netherlands: Kluwer.

Brock, R., & Goodman, G. (2013). *School sucks: Arguments for alternative education.* New York, NY: Peter Lang.

Brown, P., Lauder, H., & Ashton, D. (2011). *The global auction: The broken promises of education, jobs and incomes.* Oxford, UK: Oxford University Press.

Bruner, J. (1996). *The culture of education.* Cambridge, MA: Harvard University.

Bryk, A., & Schneider, B. (2002). *Trust in schools: A core resource for improvement.* New York, NY: Russell Sage Foundation.

Bungay, H., & Clift, S. (2010). Arts on prescription: A review of practice in the UK. *Perspectives in Public Health, 130*(6), 277–281. doi:10.1177/1757913910384050

Burawoy, M. (1991). *Ethnography unbound: Power and resistance in the modern metropolis.* Berkeley, CA: University of California Press.

Butler, J. (1990). *Gender trouble: Feminism and the subversion of identity.* New York, NY: Routledge.

Butterwick, S., & Selman, J. (2003). Deep listening in a feminist popular theatre project: Upsetting the position of audience in participatory education. *Adult Education Quarterly, 54*(1), 7–22.

Cai, Y. (2017). Bonding, bridging, and linking: Photovoice for resilience through social capital. *Natural Hazards, 88*(2), 1169–1195.

Carney, T., & Stanford, J. (2018). *The dimensions of insecure work: A factbook.* Canberra, ACT: Australia Institute. Retrieved from https://d3n8a8pro7vhmx.cloudfront.net/theausinstitute/pages/2807/attachments/original/1528337971/Insecure_Work_Factbook.pdf?1528337971

Catalano, R. F., Berglund, M. L., Ryan, J. A. M., Lonczack, H. S., & Hawkins, J. D. (2004). Positive youth development in the United States: Research findings on evaluations of positive youth development programs *Annals of the American Academy of Political and Social Science, 591*(1), 98–124. doi:10.1177/0002716203260102

Choo, S. S. (2018). Approaching twenty-first century education from a cosmopolitan perspective. *Journal of Curriculum Studies, 50*(2), 162–181. doi:10.1080/00220272.2017.1313316

Clift, S., & Camic, P. M. (Eds.). (2016). *Oxford textbook of creative arts, health, and wellbeing: International perspectives on practice, policy, and research.* Oxford, UK: Oxford University Press.

Cocke, D., Rabkin, N., Williams, J., Haft, J., & Goldbard, A. (2007). The art of social imagination: A discussion of new creative community. *Grantmakers in the Arts Reader: Ideas and Information on Arts and Culture, 18*(1), 26–31.

Cohen-Cruz, J. (2010). *Engaging performance: Theatre as call and response.* Abingdon, Oxon: Routledge.

Comber, B., Thomson, P., & Wells, M. (2001). Critical literacy finds a 'place': Writing and social action in a low-income Australian grade 2/3 classroom. *Elementary School Journal, 101*(4), 451–464.

Corbett, M. (2013). Improvisation as a curricular metaphor: Imagining education for a rural creative class. *Journal of Research in Rural Education, 28*(10), 1–13. Retrieved from http://jrre.vmhost.psu.edu/wp-content/uploads/2014/02/28-10.pdf

Corradi Fiumara, G. (2014). *The mind's affective life.* East Sussex, UK: Routledge.

Cultural Learning Alliance. (2011). *ImagineNation: The case for Cultural Learning.* London, UK: Cultural Learning Alliance.

Cultural Learning Alliance. (2017). *ImagineNation: The power of Cultural Learning.* London, UK: Cultural Learning Alliance.

curatorial intern. (2011, June 24). Relational aesthetics: The art of sociability. *New Britain Museum of American Art*. Retrieved from https://nbmaa.wordpress.com/2011/06/24/relational-aesthetics-the-art-of-sociability/

Damon, W. (2004). What is positive youth development? *Annals of the American Academy of Political and Social Science, 59*(1), 13–24. doi:10.1177/0002716203260092

Damon, W., Menon, J., & Bronk, K. C. (2003). The development of purpose during adolescence. *Applied Developmental Science, 7*(3), 119–128. doi:10.1207/S1532480XADS0703_2

Darder, A. (2011). Embodiments of public pedagogy: The art of soulful resistance. *Policy Futures in Education, 9*(6), 780–801.

Dart, J., & Davies, R. (2003). A dialogical, story-based evaluation tool: The most significant change technique. *American Journal of Evaluation, 24*(2), 137–155.

Davies, C., Knuiman, M., Wright, P. R., & Rosenberg, M. (2014). The art of being healthy: A qualitative, thematic framework for understanding the relationship between health and the arts. *BMJOpen, 4*(4), e004790. doi:10.1136/bmjopen-2014-004790

Davies, C., Pescud, M., Anwar McHenry, J., & Wright, P. R. (2016). Arts, public health and the national arts and health framework: A lexicon for health professionals. *Australian & New Zealand Journal of Public Health, 40*(4), 304–306. doi:10.1111/1753-6405.12545

Dawson, P., & Andriopoulos, C. (2017). *Managing change, creativity and innovation* (3rd ed.). Los Angeles, CA: Sage.

De los Reyes, E., & Gozemba, P. (2001). *Pockets of hope: How students and teachers change the world*. Westport, CT: Praeger.

Denzin, N. K. (2003). The call to performance. *Symbolic Interaction, 26*(1), 187–297.

Development Services Group. (2016). *Arts-based programs and arts therapies for at-risk, justice-involved, and traumatized youths*. Washington, DC: Office of Juvenile Justice and Delinquency Prevention. Retrieved from https://www.ojjdp.gov/mpg/litreviews/Arts-Based-Programs-for-Youth.pdf

Dewey, J. (1944). *Democracy and education: An introduction to the philosophy of education*. New York, NY: Free Press. (Original work published 1916)

Dewey, J. (1959). *Art as experience*. New York, NY: Capricorn Books. (Original work published 1934)

Dimitriadis, G. (2009). *Performing identity/performing culture*. New York, NY: Peter Lang.

Dissanayake, E. (1995). *Homo aestheticus: Where art comes from and why*. Seattle, WA: University of Washington Press.

Dissanayake, E. (2000). *Art and intimacy: How the arts began*. Seattle, WA: University of Washington Press.

Donaldson, S. I., Christie, C. A., & Melvin, M. M. (Eds.). (2009). *What counts as credible evidence in applied research and evaluation practice?* Thousand Oaks, CA: Sage.

Down, B., Smyth, J., & Robinson, J. (2018). *Rethinking school-to-work transitions in Australia: Young people have something to say.* Dordrecht, the Netherlands: Springer.

Ellingson, L. L., & Sotirin, P. (2019). Data engagement: A critical materialist framework for making data in qualitative research. *Qualitative Inquiry* (Advance online publication). doi:10.1177/1077800419846639

Ennis, G. M., & Tonkin, J. (2018). 'It's like exercise for your soul': How participation in youth arts activities contributes to young people's wellbeing. *Journal of Youth Studies, 21*(3), 340–359.

Eno, B. (1995, January). The big here and long now. *Essays.* Retrieved from https://longnow.org/essays/big-here-and-long-now/

Erstad, O. (2011). The learning lives of digital youth – Beyond the formal and informal. *Oxford Review of Education, 38*(1), 25–43. doi:10.1080/03054985.2011.577940

Evans, P., & Piccini, A. (2017). The regulatory aesthetics of co-production. In A. Ersoy (Ed.), *The impact of co-production: From community engagement to social justice* (pp. 99–118). Bristol, UK: Policy Press.

Evans, S., & Boyte, H. (1986). *Free spaces: The sources of democratic change in America.* Chicago, IL: University of Chicago Press.

Fahey, J., Prosser, H., & Shaw, M. (Eds.). (2015). *In the realm of the senses: Social aesthetics and the sensory dynamics of privilege.* Singapore: Springer.

Farrell, P., & McDonald, A. (2018, October 9). McDonald's accused of exploiting young workers with 'learn and churn' practice. *ABC News.* Retrieved from http://www.abc.net.au/news/2018-10-09/learn-and-churn-mcdonalds-accused-of-exploiting-young-workers/10342934

Fine, M. (2012). Resuscitating critical psychology for 'revolting' times. *Journal of Social Issues, 68*(2), 416–438.

Fine, M., Weiss, L., Centrie, C., & Roberts, R. (2000). Educating beyond the borders of schooling. *Anthropology and Education Quarterly, 31*(2), 131–151.

Finkelpearl, T. (2014). Participatory arts. In M. Kelly (Ed.), *Encyclopedia of aesthetics* (2nd ed.). Oxford, UK: Oxford University Press. Retrieved from http://www.oxfordreference.com/view/10.1093/acref/9780199747108.001.0001/acref-9780199747108-e-552

Flinders, C. (2003). *Rebalancing the world.* New York, NY: HarperCollins.

Foundation for Young Australians. (2018). *The new work order.* Melbourne, Vic: Foundation for Young Australians.

Fraser, N., Dahl, H. M., Stoltz, P., & Willig, R. (2004). Recognition, redistribution and representation in capitalist global society: An interview with Nancy Fraser. *Acta Sociologica, 47*(4), 374–382.

Freebody, P., & Luke, A. (1990). Literacies programs: Debates and demands in cultural context. *Prospect: Australian Journal of TESOL, 5*(7), 7–16.

Freire, P. (1998). *Pedagogy of freedom: Ethics, democracy, and civic courage.* New York, NY: Rowman and Littlefield.

Freire, P. (2000). *Pedagogy of the oppressed* (30th anniversary ed.). New York, NY: Continuum. (Original work published 1970)

Freire, P. (2007). *Daring to dream: Toward a pedagogy of the unfinished.* Boulder, CO: Paradigm Publishers.

Freire, P. (2014). *Pedagogy of hope: Reliving pedagogy of the oppressed.* London, UK: Bloomsbury.

Freire, P. (2016). *Pedagogy of the heart.* London, UK: Bloomsbury.

Froggett, L., & Briggs, S. (2012). Practice-near and practice-distant methods in human services research. *Journal of Research Practice, 8*(2). Retrieved from http://jrp.icaap.org/index.php/jrp/article/view/318/276

Furlong, A., & Cartmel, F. (1997). *Young people and social change: Individualization and risk in late modernity.* Buckingham, UK: Open University Press.

Gallagher, C. W. (2002). *Radical departures: Composition and progressive pedagogies.* Urbana, IL: NCTE.

Gee, J., Hull, G., & Lankshear, C. (1996). *The new work order: Behind the language of the new capitalism.* St Leonards, NSW: Allen & Unwin.

Giroux, H. (2012). *Education and the crisis of public values: Challenging the assault on teachers, students and public education.* New York, NY: Peter Lang.

Goldbard, A. (2013). *The culture of possibility: Art, artists & the future.* Richmond, CA: Waterlight Press.

Goldbard, A. (2017). Belonging as a cultural right. *Othering and Belonging, 2,* 15–31. Retrieved from http://www.otheringandbelonging.org/belonging-cultural-right/

Gonzalez, N., & Moll, L. C. (2002). *Cruzando el Puente*: Building bridges to funds of knowledge. *Educational Policy, 16*(4), 623–641.

Gonzalez, N., Moll, L. C., & Amanti, C. (Eds.). (2006). *Funds of knowledge: Theorizing practices in households, communities, and classrooms.* New York, NY: Routledge.

Gordon, S., Benner, P., & Noddings, N. (Eds.). (1996). *Caregiving: Readings in knowledge, practice, ethics, and politics.* Philadelphia, PA: University of Philadelphia Press.

Gorz, A. (1997). *Reclaiming work: Beyond the wage-based society.* Cambridge, UK: Polity Press.

Granger, D. A. (2006). *John Dewey, Robert Persig, and the art of living: Revisioning aesthetic education.* New York, NY: Palgrave/MacMillan.

Graves, J. B. (2005). *Cultural democracy: The arts, community & the public purpose.* Urbana, IL: University of Illinois Press.

Green, J. (1999). *Deep democracy: Community, diversity, and transformation.* Lanham, MD: Rowman & Littlefield.

Greene, M. (1977). Toward wide-awakeness: An argument for the arts and humanities in education. *Teachers College Record, 79*(1), 119–125.

Greene, M. (1995). *Releasing the imagination: Essays on education, the arts, and social change.* San Francisco, CA: Jossey-Bass.

Greene, M. (2001a). Foreword. In G. Huduk & P. Kihn (Eds.), *Labeling: Pedagogy and politics* (pp. xvi–xvii). London, UK: Routledge/Falmer.

Greene, M. (2001b). *Variations on a blue guitar: The Lincoln Centre Institute lectures on aesthetic education.* New York, NY: Teachers College Press.

Greene, M. (2003). In search of a critical pedagogy. In A. Darder, M. Baltodano, & R. D. Torres (Eds.), *The critical pedagogy reader* (pp. 97–112). New York, NY: Routledge.

Greene, M. (2005). Teaching in a moment of crisis: The space of imagination. *New Educator, 1*(2), 77–80.

Greene, M. (2010). Prologue to art, social imagination and action. *Journal of Educational Controversy, 5*(1). Retrieved from https://cedar.wwu.edu/jec/vol5/iss1/2

Grossberg, L. (2005). *Caught in the crossfire: Kids, politics and America's future.* Boulder, CO: Paradigm.

Gruenewald, D. (2003a). Foundations of place: Multidisciplinary framework for place-based education. *American Educational Research Journal, 40*(3), 619–654.

Gruenewald, D. (2003b). The best of both worlds: A critical pedagogy of place. *Educational Researcher, 32*(4), 3–12.

Grumet, M. (2004). No one learns alone. In N. Rabkin & R. Redmond (Eds.), *Putting the arts in the picture: Reframing education in the 21st century* (pp. 49–80). Chicago, IL: Center for Arts Policy, Columbia College Chicago.

Halpern, D. (2010). *The hidden wealth of nations.* Cambridge, UK: Polity Press.

Halpern-Meekin, S. (2019). *Social poverty.* New York, NY: NYU Press.

Harvey, D. (2003). *The new imperialism.* Oxford, UK: Oxford University Press.

Harvey, D. (2007). *A brief history of neoliberalism.* New York, NY: Oxford University Press.

Hawkes, J. (2001). *The fourth pillar of sustainability: Culture's essential role in public planning.* Melbourne, Vic: Cultural Development Network (Vic.) in association with Common Ground Publishing.

Helguera, P. (2011). *Education for socially engaged art: A materials and techniques handbook.* New York, NY: Jorge Pinto Books.

Hempel-Jorgensen, A. (2015). Learner agency and social justice: What can creative pedagogy contribute to socially just pedagogies? *Pedagogy, Culture & Society, 23*(4), 531–554. doi:10.1080/14681366.2015.1082497

Holden, J. (2010). *Culture and class.* London, UK: Counterpoint.

Holt, M. (2015). Transformation of the aesthetic: Art as participatory design. *Design and Culture, 7*(2), 143–165. doi:10.1080/17547075.2015.1051781

Horsfall, D. (2008). Performing communit(y)ies. *Forum Qualitative Sozialforschung/ Forum: Qualitative Social Research, 9*(2), art 57. Retrieved from http://www.qualitative-research.net/fqs-texte/a5b6c7/08-2-57-e.htm

hooks, b. (2003). *Teaching community: A pedagogy of hope*. New York, NY: Routledge.

hooks, b. (2009). *Belonging: A culture of place*. New York, NY: Routledge.

Hudak, G. (2001). On what is labeled 'playing': Locating the 'true' in education. In G. Huduk & P. Kihn (Eds.), *Labeling: Pedagogy and politics* (pp. 9–26). London, UK: Routledge/Falmer.

Huss, E., & Bos, E. (Eds.). (2019). *Art in social work practice: Theory and practice: International perspectives*. Abingdon, Oxon, UK: Routledge.

Hutchinson, J. (2004). Democracy needs strangers, and we are them. In C. Bingham & A. Sidorkin (Eds.), *No education without relation* (pp. 73–89). New York, NY: Peter Lang.

Ibrahim, A., & Steinberg, S. R. (Eds.). (2014). *Critical youth studies reader*. New York, NY: Peter Lang.

Irvine, J. (2018, June 22). Young and out: Australia's hidden scourge of youth unemployment. *The Age*. Retrieved from https://www.theage.com.au/business/the-economy/young-and-out-Australia-s-hidden-scourge-of-youth-unemployment-20180622-p4zn4k.html?btis

Ivey, B. (2008). *Arts, inc: How greed and neglect have destroyed our cultural rights*. Berkeley, CA: University of California Press.

Jenkins, H., Shresthova, S., Gamber-Thompson, L., Kligler-Vilenchik, N., & Zimmerman, A. M. (2016). *By any media necessary: The new youth activism*. New York, NY: NYU Press.

Jensen, A., Stickley, T., & Edgley, A. (2016). The perspectives of people who use mental health services engaging with arts and cultural activities. *Mental Health and Social Inclusion, 20*(3), 180–186. doi:10.1108/MHSI-02-2016-0011

Jericho, G. (2018, August 28). Long-term unemployment rates show the jobs picture is not so rosy. *The Guardian*. Retrieved from https://www.theguardia.com/business/grogonomics/2018/aug/28/long-term-unemployment-rates-show-the-jobs-picture-is-not-rosy

Jessop, G. (2016). Let them flourish: Meeting the complex needs of vulnerable young people. *Parity, 29*(1), 37–38. Retrieved from http://search.informit.com.au/documentSummary;dn=979949354361324;res=IELHSS

Jones, S. (2007, July 26). *Building cultural literacy: Museums and intercultural collaboration*. Paper presented at New Collaboration, New Benefits – Transnational Museum Collaboration Conference, Shanghai, China. Retrieved from http://apo.org.au/node/15733

Jones, S. (2010). *Culture shock*. London, UK: Demos.

Karlgren, K., Paavola, S., & Beatrice Ligorio, M. (2020). Introduction: What are knowledge work practices in education? How can we study and promote them? *Research Papers in Education, 1*, 1–7.

Kay, A. (2000). Art and community development: The role the arts have in regenerating communities. *Community Development Journal, 35*(4), 414–424. doi:10.1093/cdj/35.4.414

Kester, G. (2011). *The one and the many: Contemporary collaborative art in a global context.* Durham, NC: Duke University Press.

Kilroy, A., Garner, C., Parkinson, C., Kagan, C., & Senior, P. (2008). *Invest to save: Arts in health evaluation, exploring the impact of creativity, culture and the arts, on health and wellbeing.* Manchester, UK: Manchester Metropolitan University. Retrieved from http://www.artsandhealth.ie/wp-content/uploads/2011/09/Invest-to-Save-Arts-in-Health-Evaluation.pdf

Kincheloe, J. (1995). *Toil and trouble: Good work, smart workers, and the integration of academic and vocational education.* New York, NY: Peter Lang.

Kincheloe, J. (1999). *How do we tell the workers? The socioeconomic foundations of work and vocational education.* Boulder, CO: Westview Press.

Kohl, H. (1994). *'I won't learn from you' and other thoughts on creative maladjustment.* New York, NY: New Press.

Korsgaard, C. M. (2009). *Self-constitution: Agency, identity, and integrity.* Oxford, UK: Oxford University Press.

Langer, S. K. (1952). *Feeling and form: A theory of art developed from 'Philosophy in a new key'.* New York, NY: Charles Scribner's Sons.

Lawrence-Lightfoot, S. (2005). Reflections on portraiture: A dialogue between art and science. *Qualitative Inquiry, 11*(3), 3–15. doi:10.1177/1077800404270955

Lawrence-Lightfoot, S., & Hoffman Davis, J. (1997). *The art and science of portraiture.* San Francisco, CA: Jossey-Bass.

Ledwith, M., & Springett, J. (2010). *Participatory practice: Community-based action for transformative change.* Bristol, UK: Policy Press.

Lennie, J., & Tacchi, J. (2013). *Evaluating communication for development: A framework for social change.* Abingdon, Oxon, UK: Routledge.

Leonard, R. H., & Kilkelly, A. (2006). *Performing communities: Grassroots ensemble theaters deeply rooted in eight U.S. communities.* Oakland, CA: New Village Press.

Lewis, F. (2013). *Participatory art-making and civic engagement.* Washington, DC: Animating Democracy. Retrieved from http://animatingdemocracy.org/resource/participatory-art-making-and-civic-engagement

Luksha, P., Cubista, J., Laszlo, A., Popovich, M., & Ninenko, I. (2018). *Educational ecosystems for societal transformation.* Amersfoort, the Netherlands: Global Education Futures.

MacDougall, D. (2006). *The corporeal image: Film, ethnography and the senses.* Princeton, NJ: Princeton University Press.

Macrine, S. (Ed.). (2009). *Critical pedagogy in uncertain times: Hope and possibilities.* New York, NY: Palgrave Macmillan.

Mahon, M. (2000). The visible evidence of cultural producers. *Annual Review of Anthropology, 29*, 467–492.

Malin, H. (2015). Arts participation as a context for youth purpose. *Studies in Art Education, 56*(3), 268–280. doi:10.1080/00393541.2015.11518968

Marcus, G. E. (1998). *Ethnography through thick and thin*. Princeton, NJ: Princeton University Press.

Margonis, F. (2004). From student resistance to educative engagement: A case study in building powerful student–teacher relationships. In C. Bingham & A. Sidorkin (Eds.), *No education without relation* (pp. 39–53). New York, NY: Peter Lang.

Markusen, A., & Gadwa, A. (2010). *Creative placemaking*. Washington, DC: National Endowment for the Arts.

Marmot, M. (2014). *Review of the social determinants of the health divide in the WHO European region*. Copenhagen, Denmark: World Health Organization. Retrieved from http://www.euro.who.int/__data/assets/pdf_file/0004/251878/Review-of-social-determinants-and-the-health-divide-in-the-WHO-European-Region-FINAL-REPORT.pdf

Martin, J. L. (2011). *The explanation of social action*. Oxford, UK: Oxford University Press.

Matarasso, F. (2019). *A restless art: How participation won, and why it matters*. London, UK: Calouste Gulbenkian Foundation.

Matarasso, F. (2020, January 4). Culture is a right, not a solution. *François Matarasso thinking about culture as if people mattered blog*. Retrieved from https://parliamentofdreams.com/2020/01/04/culture-is-a-right-not-a-solution/

McLaren, P. (1995). *Critical pedagogy and predatory culture: Oppositional politics in a postmodern era*. New York, NY: Routledge.

McLaren, P., & Farahmandpur, R. (2005). *Teaching against global capitalism and the new imperialism*. Oxford, UK: Rowman and Littlefield.

Miles, M. B., Huberman, A. M., & Saldaña, J. (2014). *Qualitative data analysis: A methods sourcebook* (3rd ed.). Thousand Oaks, CA: Sage.

Miller, R., Looney, J., & Siemens, G. (2011). *Assessment competency: Knowing what you know & learning analytics: It's time for a breakthrough, Promethean thinking deeper*. Retrieved from http://www.21digitalclass.com/uploads/4/7/2/9/47298253/c2_-_assesment_competency_-_knowing_what_you_know_and_learning_analytics.pdf

Miller, T. (2007). Culture, dislocation, and citizenship. In E. Elliott, J. Payne, & P. Ploesch (Eds.), *Global migration, social change, and cultural transformation* (pp. 165–186). New York, NY: Palgrave Macmillan.

Mills, C. W. (1971). *The sociological imagination*. New York, NY: Penguin Books. (Original work published 1959)

Montgomery, D. (2014). *Creative youth development movement takes hold*. New York, NY: National Guild for Community Arts Education.

Moorfield-Lang, H. (2010). Arts voices: Middle school students and the relationships of the arts to their motivation and self-efficacy. *Qualitative Report, 15*(1), 1–17. Retrieved from www.nova.edu/ssss/QR/QR15-1/moorefield-lang.pdf

Morse, J. M., Swanson, J., & Kuzel, A. J. (Eds.). (2001). *The nature of qualitative evidence.* Thousand Oaks, CA: Sage.

Mowlah, A., Niblett, V., Blackburn, J., & Harris, M. (2014). *The value of arts and culture to people and society: An evidence review.* Manchester, UK: Arts Council England.

National Academies of Sciences, Engineering, and Medicine. (2019). *The promise of adolescence: Realizing opportunity for all youth.* Washington, DC: National Academies Press.

New London Group. (1996). A pedagogy of multiliteracies: Designing social futures. *Harvard Educational Review, 66*(1), 60–92.

Nielsen, P. (2015). *Social aesthetics – What is it?* Retrieved from https://books.ub.uni-heidelberg.de/arthistoricum/reader/download/49/49-17-264-1-10-20151214.pdf

Noddings, N. (1984). *Caring, a feminine approach to ethics and moral education.* Berkeley, CA: University of California Press.

Nussbaum, M. C. (2003). Capabilities as fundamental entitlements: Sen and social justice. *Feminist Economics, 9*(2–3), 33–59.

Nussbaum, M. C. (2011). *Creating capabilities: The human development approach.* Cambridge, MA: Belknap Press of Harvard University Press.

Nutley, S., Powell, A., & Davies, H. (2013). *What counts as good evidence?* London, UK: Alliance for Useful Evidence. Retrieved from http://www.alliance4usefulevidence.org/assets/What-Counts-as-Good-Evidence-WEB.pdf

Oakes, J. (2005). *Keeping track: How schools structure inequality.* New Haven, CT: Yale University Press. (First published 1985)

Oakes, J., Rogers, J., with Lipton, M. (2006). *Learning power: Organizing for education and justice.* New York, NY: Teachers College Press.

Offer, A. (2011). *The challenge of affluence: Self-control and well-being in the United States and Britain since 1950.* Oxford, UK: Oxford University Press.

Ohanian, S. (1999). *One size fits few: The folly of educational standards.* Portsmouth. UK: Heinemann.

Ozden Firat, B., & Kuryel, A. (Eds.). (2011). *Cultural activism: Practices, dilemmas and possibilities.* Amsterdam, the Netherlands: Rodopi.

Patulny, R. V., & Svendsen, G. L. H. (2007). Exploring the social capital grid: Bonding, bridging, qualitative, quantitative. *International Journal of Sociology and Social Policy, 27*(1–2), 32–51. doi:10.1108/01443330710722742

Pawson, R., & Tilley, N. (1997). *Realistic evaluation.* London, UK: Sage.

Pinar, W. F. (Ed.). (1998). *The passionate mind of Maxine Greene: 'I am … not yet'.* London, UK: Falmer Press.

Pincock, S. (2008, August 14). Food bowl to dustbowl? *ABC Science.* Retrieved from https://www.abc.net.au/science/articles/2008/08/14/2335296.htm

Polanyi, M. (1966). *The tacit dimension.* London, UK: Routledge and Kegan Paul.

Preskill, H., & Gopal, S. (2014). *Evaluating complexity: Propositions for improving practice.* Boston, MA: FSG. Retrieved from http://www.issuelab.org/resource/evaluating_complexity_propositions_for_improving_practice

Proweller, A. (2000). Re-writing/righting lives: Voices of pregnant and parenting teenagers in an alternative school. In L. Weiss & M. Fine (Eds.), *Construction sites: Excavating race, class and gender among urban youth* (pp. 100–120). New York, NY: Teachers College Press.

Putnam, R. D. (2000). *Bowling alone: The collapse and revival of American community.* New York, NY: Simon & Schuster.

Qvortrup, L. (2003). *The hypercomplex society.* New York, NY: Peter Lang.

Radbourne, J., Glow, H., & Johanson, K. (Eds.). (2013). *The audience experience: A critical analysis of audiences in the performing arts.* Bristol, UK: Intellect.

Rankin, S. (2014). Soggy biscuit: Invisible lives – or the emperor's new social work? *Griffith Review, 44,* 11–32.

Rankin, S. (2018). *Cultural justice and the right to thrive.* Sydney, NSW: Currency Press.

Rao, V., & Walton, M. (2004). Conclusion: Implications of a cultural lens for public policy and development thought. In V. Rao & M. Walton (Eds.), *Culture and public education* (pp. 359–372). Stanford, CA: Stanford University Press.

Rasmussen, B., & Wright, P. R. (2001). The theatre workshop as educational space: How imagined reality is voiced and conceived. *International Journal of Education & the Arts, 2*(2). Retrieved from http://www.ijea.org/v2n2/index.html

Rios, V. (2011). *Punished: Policing the lives of black and Latino boys.* New York, NY: NYU Press.

Risjord, M. (2019). Middle-range theories as models: New criteria for analysis and evaluation. *Nursing Philosophy, 20*(1). doi:10.1111/nup.12225

Rittel, H. W., & Webber, M. M. (1973). Dilemmas in a general theory of planning. *Policy Sciences, 4*(2), 155–169.

Robinson, B., & Kutner, M. (2018). Spinoza and the affective turn: A return to the philosophical origins of affect. *Qualitative Inquiry, 25*(2), 111–117.

Roerich, N. (2010). Call to world unity. In P. Barenboim & N. Sidiqi (Eds.), *Bruges, the bridge between civilizations. To the 75th anniversary of the Roerich Pact* (pp. 47–50). Moscow, Russia: Letny Sad.

Rogers, C. (1980). *A way of being.* Boston, MA: Houghton Mifflin.

Rose, M. (1989). *Lives on the boundary: The struggles and achievements of America's underprepared.* New York, NY: Free Press.

Ross, A. (2008). The new geography of work: Power to the precarious? *Theory, Culture and Society, 25*(7–8), 31–49.

Said, E. (1993). *Culture and imperialism*. New York, NY: Random House.

Saldaña, J. (2016). *The coding manual for qualitative researchers* (3rd ed.). Thousand Oaks, CA: Sage.

Schaffer Bacon, B., & Korza, P. (2010). Articulating the civic and social impacts of the arts: The arts & civic impact initiative at Americans for the Arts. *CultureWork, 10*(4). Retrieved from http://pages.uoregon.edu/culturwk/culturework50.html

Schneekloth, L., & Shibley, R. (1995). *Placemaking: The art and practice of building communities*. New York, NY: John Wiley & Sons.

Schumacher, E. F. (1973). *Small is beautiful: A study of economics as if people mattered*. London, UK: Blond & Briggs.

Seidman, I. (2013). *Interviewing as qualitative research* (4th ed.). New York, NY: Teachers College Press.

Seligman, M. E. P. (1972). Learned helplessness. *Annual Review of Medicine, 23*, 407–412.

Sellar, S. (2009).The responsible uncertainty of pedagogy. *Discourse: Studies in the Cultural Politics of Education, 30*(3), 347–360.

Sellar, S. (2012). 'It's all about relationships': Hesitation, friendship and pedagogical assemblage. *Discourse: Studies in the Cultural Politics of Education, 33*(1), 61–74.

Sen, A. (1992). *Inequality re-examined*. Cambridge, MA: Harvard University Press.

Sen, A. (1999). *Development as freedom*. New York, NY: Knopf.

Senge, P. M. (2018). Foreword. In P. Luksha, J. Cubista, A. Laszlo, M. Popovich, & I. Ninenko (Eds.), *Educational ecosystems for societal transformation* (pp. iv–vii). Amersfoort, the Netherlands: Global Education Futures.

Sennett, R. (2006). *The culture of new capitalism*. New Haven, CT: Yale University Press.

Sharpe, B. (2010). *Economies of life: Patterns of health and wealth*. Aberdore, Fife: Triarchy Press.

Shor, I. (1992). *Empowering education: Critical teaching for social change*. Chicago, IL: University of Chicago Press.

Shusterman, R. (2004). Somaesthetics and education: Exploring the terrain. In L. Bresler (Ed.), *Knowing bodies, moving minds: Towards embodied teaching and learning* (pp. 51–60). Dordrecht, the Netherlands: Kluwer.

Silbereisen, R. K., & Lerner, R. M. (2007). *Approaches to positive youth development*. Thousand Oaks, CA: Sage.

Smyth. J. (2016). Youth insecurity in schools: What's going on with class? *International Studies in Sociology of Education, 26*(2), 211–227.

Smyth, J., Down, B., & McInerney, P. (2010). *'Hanging in with kids' in tough times: Engagement in context of educational in the relational school*. New York, NY: Peter Lang.

Smyth, J., & Hattam, R. (2004). *'Dropping out', drifting off, being excluded: Becoming somebody without school*. New York, NY: Peter Lang.

Smyth, J., & McInerney, P. (2012). *From silent witnesses to active agents: Student voice in re-engaging with learning*. New York, NY: Peter Lang.

Soffel, J. (2016, March 10). What are the 21st-century skills every student needs? *World Economic Forum*. Retrieved from https://www.weforum.org/agenda/2016/03/21st-century-skills-future-jobs-students/

Somerville, M., Davies, B., Power, K., Gannon, S., & de Carteret, P. (2011). *Place, pedagogy, change*. Rotterdam, the Netherlands: Sense.

Somerville, M., & Perkins, T. (2003). Border work in the contact zone: Thinking Indigenous/non-Indigenous collaboration spatially. *Journal of Intercultural Studies, 24*(3), 253–266. doi:10.1080/0725686032000172597

Sometimes, B., & Kelly, A. (2010). Ngapartji Ngapartji: Indigenous language in the arts. In J. Hobson, K. Lowe, S. Poetsch, & M. Walsh (Eds.), *Re-awakening languages: Theory and practice in the revitalisation of Australia's Indigenous languages* (pp. 84–89). Sydney, NSW: Sydney University Press.

Spring, J. (2015). *Economization of education: Human capital, global corporations, skills-based schooling*. New York, NY: Routledge.

Stam, R. (2015). *Keywords in subversive film/media aesthetics*. Chichester, West Sussex, UK: John Wiley & Sons.

Standing, G. (2011). *The precariat: The new dangerous class*. London, UK: Bloomsbury.

Stanton-Salazar, R. (1997). A social capital framework for understanding the socialization of racial minority children and youths. *Harvard Educational Review, 67*(1), 1–40.

Steinberg, S., & Kincheloe, J. (1998). *Students as researchers: Creating classrooms that matter*. London, UK: Falmer.

Stern, M. J., & Seifert, S. C. (2009). *Civic engagement and the arts: Issues of conceptualization and measurement*. Washington, DC: Animating Democracy.

Stevenson, L. M. (2014). *Setting the agenda: National summit on creative youth development*. New York, NY: National Guild for Community Arts Education.

Stewart, E. (2018, June 28). The PaTH scheme is a farcical way to tackle youth unemployment. *The Age*. Retrieved from https://www.theage.com.au/business/workplace/the-path-scheme-is-farcical-way-to-tackle-youth-unemployment-20180628-p4zoaw.html

Stickley, T., & Clift, S. (Eds.). (2017). *Arts, health and wellbeing: A theoretical inquiry for practice*. Newcastle upon Tyne, UK: Cambridge Scholars Publishing.

Stuckey, H. L., & Nobel, J. (2010). The connection between art, healing, and public health. *American Journal of Public Health, 100*(2), 254–263. doi:10.2105/AJPH.2008.156497

Swadener, B. (1995). Children and families 'at promise': Deconstructing the discourse of risk. In B. Swadener & S. Lubeck (Eds.), *Children and families 'at promise': Deconstructing the discourse of risk* (pp. 17–49). Albany, NY: State University of New York Press.

Swan, P. (2013). Promoting social inclusion through community arts. *Mental Health and Social Inclusion, 17*(1), 19–26.

Szreter, S., & Woolcock, M. (2004). Health by association? Social capital, social theory, and the political economy of public health. *International Journal of Epidemiology, 33*(4), 650–667.

Theobold, P. (1997). *Teaching the commons: Place, pride and the renewal of community.* Oxford, UK: Westview Press.

Theobold, P., & Curtiss, J. (2000). Communities as curricula. *Forum for Applied Research and Public Policy, 15*(1), 106–111.

Thomson, P., Hall, C., Earl, L., & Geppert, C. (2019). Towards an arts education for cultural citizenship. In S. Riddle & M. W. Apple (Eds.), *Re-imagining education for democracy* (pp. 174–189). Abingdon, Oxon, UK: Routledge.

Tulloch, J. (1999). *Performing culture: Stories of expertise and the everyday.* London, UK: Sage.

Turner, E. (2012). *Communitas: The anthropology of collective joy.* New York, NY: Palgrave McMillan.

UNESCO. (2018). *The right to culture: Questions and answers.* Paris, France: UNESCO. Retrieved from http://www.unesco.org/culture/culture-sector-knowledge-management-tools/10_Info%20Sheet_Right%20to%20Culture.pdf

UNESCO. (2019). *Migration and inclusive societies.* Retrieved from https://en.unesco.org/themes/fostering-rights-inclusion/migration

United Nations. (1948). *Universal declaration of human rights.* Retrieved from https://www.un.org/en/universal-declaration-human-rights/index.html

United Nations. (2006). *Social justice in an open world: The role of the united nations.* New York, NY: United Nations. Retrieved from http://www.un.org/esa/socdev/documents/ifsd/SocialJustice.pdf

Vagle, M. D. (Ed.). (2012). *Not a stage! A critical re-conception of young adolescent education.* New York, NY: Peter Lang.

Valencia, R. (2010). *Dismantling contemporary deficit thinking: Educational thought and practice.* New York, NY: Routledge.

van Staveren, I., & Knorringa, P. (2007). Unpacking social capital in economic development: How social relations matter. *Review of Social Economy, 65*(1), 107–135.

Vinson, T. (2007). *Dropping off the edge: The distribution of disadvantage in Australia.* Richmond, Vic: Jesuit Social Services and Catholic Social Services Australia.

Vinson, T. (2009). *Social inclusion: Intergenerational disadvantage.* Barton, ACT: Commonwealth of Australia.

Wade, M. (2018, November 4). Financial crisis hit young men hard – and they're yet to recover. *The Age.* Retrieved from http://www.theage.com.au/business/the-economy/financial-crisis-hit-young-men-hard-and-they-re-yet-to-recover-20181102-p50dpd.html?btis

Walker, M. (2006). Towards a capability-based theory of social justice for education policy-making. *Journal of Education Policy, 21*(2), 163–185.

Ware, V.-A. (2014). *Supporting healthy communities through arts programs* (Closing the Gap Clearinghouse Resource Sheet No. 28). Canberra, ACT: Australian Institute of Health and Welfare.

Wenger, E. (1998). *Communities of practice: Learning, meaning, and identity.* Cambridge, UK: Cambridge University Press.

Wexler, P. (1992). *Becoming somebody: Toward a social psychology of school.* London, UK: Falmer Press.

Wheelahan, L. (2017). Rethinking skills development: Moving beyond competency-based training. In J. Buchanan, D. Finegold, K. Mayhew, & C. Warhurst (Eds.), *The Oxford handbook of skills and training.* Oxford, UK: Oxford University Press.

White, M. (2004). Arts in mental health for social inclusion: Towards a framework for programme evaluation. In J. Cowling (Ed.), *For art's sake: Society and the arts in the 21st century* (pp. 75–99). London, UK: Institute for Public Policy Research.

White, M. (2009). *Arts development in community health: A social tonic.* Abingdon, UK: Radcliffe.

Wigginton, E. (1986). *Sometimes a shining moment: The foxfire experience.* Garden City, NY: Anchor Books.

Wilson, N., Gross, J., & Bull, A. (2017). *Towards cultural democracy: Promoting cultural capabilities for everyone.* London, UK: King's College London. Retrieved from https://www.kcl.ac.uk/Cultural/-/Projects/Towards-cultural-democracy.aspx

Woolcock, M., & Narayan, D. (2000). Social capital: Implications for development theory, research, and policy. *The World Bank Research Observer, 15*(2), 225–249.

World Health Organization. (2020). Social determinants of health. *World Health Organization.* Retrieved from https://www.who.int/social_determinants/sdh_definition/en/

Wright, P. R. (2009). *It's like thinking with both sides of your brain. BIG hART's LUCKY project: An imaginative intervention.* Perth, WA: Murdoch University. Retrieved from http://researchrepository.murdoch.edu.au/2602/

Wright, P. R. (2011). Agency, intersubjectivity and drama education: The power to be and do more. In S. Schonmann (Ed.), *Key concepts in theatre/drama education* (pp. 111–115). Rotterdam, the Netherlands: Sense.

Wright, P. R. (2012). Performing 'hope': Authentic story, change and transformation in teacher education. In B. Down & J. Smyth (Eds.), *Critical voices in teacher education* (pp. 211–221). Dordrecht, the Netherlands: Springer.

Wright, P. R. (2017). Ways of being, belonging and becoming: Arts practice, the relational and cultural learning. In S. Wiebe, E. Lyle, P. R. Wright, K. Dark, M. McLarnon, & L. Day (Eds.), *Ways of being in teaching: Conversations and reflections* (pp. 33–46). Rotterdam, the Netherlands: Sense.

Wright, P. R. (2020). Towards a critical arts practice. In S. R. Steinberg & B. Down (Eds.), *The Sage handbook of critical pedagogies* (pp. 1269–1278). London, UK: Sage.

Wright, P. R., Davies, C., Haseman, B., Down, B., White, M., & Rankin, S. (2013). Arts practice and disconnected youth in Australia: Impact and domains of change. *Arts & Health, 5*(3), 190–203.

Wright, P. R., Down, B., Rankin, S., Haseman, B., White, M., & Davies, C. (2016). *BIG hART: Art, equity and community for people, place and policy.* Perth, WA: Murdoch University. Retrieved from http://researchrepository.murdoch.edu.au/id/eprint/35589

Wright, P. R., & Palmer, D. (2007). *People now know me for something positive: An Evaluation of BIG hART's work at the John Northcott Estate.* Perth, WA: Murdoch University.

Wright, P. R., & Pascoe, R. (2015). Eudaimonia and creativity: The art of human flourishing. *Cambridge Journal of Education, 45*(3), 295–306. doi:10.1080/0305764X.2013.855172

Zournazi, M. (2002). *Hope: New philosophies for change.* London, UK: Routledge.

Index

Printed in the United States
By Bookmasters